# FINDING MERLIN

# FINDING
# MERLIN

## *A HANDBOOK*

*for the human development*

*journey in our new*

*organisational*

*world*

✽

## KATE COWIE

*with a foreword by* TED TSCHUDY
*contributions from* SUE HOLLINGSWORTH
*and an afterword by* M. FRANCES BALDWIN

Marshall Cavendish
Business

Copyright © Kate Cowie 2012

Published by Marshall Cavendish Business
An imprint of Marshall Cavendish International

1 New Industrial Road
Singapore 536196
genrefsales@sg.marshallcavendish.com
www.marshallcavendish.com/genref

Marshall Cavendish is a trademark of Times Publishing Limited

Other Marshall Cavendish offices:
Marshall Cavendish Corporation, 99 White Plains Road, Tarrytown
NY 10591–9001, USA ◆ Marshall Cavendish International (Thailand) Co Ltd,
253 Asoke, 12th Floor, Sukhumvit 21 Road, Klongtoey Nua, Wattana, Bangkok 10110,
Thailand ◆ Marshall Cavendish (Malaysia) Sdn Bhd, Times Subang, Lot 46, Subang Hi-Tech
Industrial Park, Batu Tiga, 40000 Shah Alam, Selangor Darul Ehsan, Malaysia

A CIP record for this book is available from the British Library

ISBN 978–981–4302–74–6

Printed and bound by CPI Group (UK) Ltd, Croydon, CR0 4YY

# CONTENTS

# Science, Myth and Metaphor

## Growing the Self in Today's Organisations

❧

*The changing context for human and
professional development.*

Human development in organisations is being redefined in what
Tom Friedman so cogently described as our "flat world". The
flat world is speed, 24-hour 'always on' business processes, and
instant communication via Blackberry, iPhone, Tweets and a
growing number of social communication technologies. In the flat
world, global competition is multiple diverse stakeholders, hyper-
competition, disruptive technologies, tipping points and feedback
cycles that quickly reward success and punish failure. Old concepts, like the hierarchy of needs, and Theory X and Theory Y,
seem somehow incomplete and 'long in the tooth' in an age that so
often links its metrics for human value directly to the bottom line.
The flat world is an exciting, challenging and sometimes risky
world in which to live and work. Kate Cowie, through science,
mythology and metaphor, explores the nature of human development in contemporary organisations, and how to do it.

In the flat world, human and professional development are
increasingly conjoined. An underlying premise of Cowie's thinking is that one cannot be an accomplished professional in the flat
world without also bringing a highly developed 'whole' Self to the
work. Accordingly, she offers a foundational framework for finding our way towards purposeful human development. She lays the
groundwork for an informed practice of human development in
contemporary organisations and links it to professional success.
It is a timely perspective and a substantial contribution to our
efforts to make work life meaningful in the flat world.

*The challenge of development in a flat world.*

Organisational life in the flat world is demanding. It is fully engaging and often exhausting. High performance demands the best of human capabilities – technical excellence, emotional intelligence, nuanced leadership, imagination, inspiration, smart risk-taking, broad vision, courage, and the ability to learn from successes and mistakes. Far-reaching ecologies of interdependence among organisations, the environment, finance, and personal and family life require vision and sensitivity to the second- and third-order impacts of organisational action. Higher-order functioning is not just valuable – it is critical for survival in the flat world.

Paradoxically, driven by the demands of their corporate environments, flat-world organisations are often inhospitable petri dishes for human development and growth. In the industrial, round world of the past, life-long employment was assumed and investments in human and professional development were seen as integral to long-term success. Human resource departments took responsibility for the short- and long-term development of individuals to serve corporate needs. There was often time and money for experiments in learning, sometimes even for play. In the flat world, employer and employee make no promises for the long term. Investments in human development are assessed based on their marginal contributions to profits. In the flat world, organisations strive to be 'lean' and human resource departments manage 'human capital'. Time is truly money in the flat world, and more apt to be spent by employee and employer alike to meet unyielding short term demands rather than invested for the less pressing, longer-term benefits of human growth. Individual contributors and leaders are too often sucked into the corporate vortex. As a colleague, Earl T. Braxton, characterises it, they get "too far in", unable to maintain the perspective (and position) that allows for the capability to be effective managers of organisational purpose, strategy and execution.

*The metaphors we live in.*

One of the useful insights of the post-modern focus on narrative is the notion that we live our lives in metaphor. It is a provocative proposition. George Lakoff and Mark Johnson describe the power of metaphor in our lives:

"Metaphor is for most people a device of the poetic imagination and the rhetorical flourish – a matter of extraordinary rather than ordinary language. Moreover, metaphor is typically viewed as characteristic of language alone, a matter of words rather than thought or action. For this reason, most people think they can get along perfectly well without metaphor. We have found, on the contrary, that metaphor is pervasive in everyday life, not just in language, but in thought and action. Our ordinary conceptual system, in terms of which we both think and act, is fundamentally metaphorical in nature.

"The concepts that govern our thought are not just matters of the intellect. They also govern our everyday functioning, down to the most mundane details. Our concepts structure what we perceive, how we get around in the world, and how we relate to other people...."†

Lakoff and Johnson's work with metaphor suggests a caution, and a possibility. The caution: lacking awareness of the metaphor in our lives, we risk living on auto-pilot, programmed with the software of our particular historical epoch. The possibility: mindful of metaphor's influence on our life experience, we can make it a friend to our desire for self-development, a window on how we can reflect upon, and reshape, the language we live by. Cowie offers us the opportunity to use the powers of metaphor in mythology – linked to a science-grounded framework – to support our own journey of self-understanding and development.

† *Metaphors We Live By*, by George Lakoff and Mark Johnson (Chicago and London: The University of Chicago Press, 1980), p 3.

Gareth Morgan shows us the reflective power of metaphor as a means to understand organisations. *Images of Organizations*, his classic work on organisation theory, has helped students of organisations see multiple dimensions of organisational life through metaphorical lenses. For example, he presents provocative pictures of organisations as machines, brains, psychic prisons and instruments of domination. In a later book, *Imaginization: the Art of Creative Management*, he illustrates how we can play with our metaphors – extending, reshaping and reframing them to discover new possibilities for understanding and action.

The flat world has found in business and capitalism a common language. Its underlying assumptions serve as universal indicators of individual and corporate success and progress towards the collective 'good'. We utilise technology and financial and human capital to produce products and services that are purchased by customers who are categorised in market segments. We focus on profit, competitive position, business strategy and the bottom line. Indicators of personal success are higher status, more responsibility, and larger salaries. The language of contemporary business, like the organisations it reflects, is lean! It is bereft of the range, the colour, the density of the enriching, generative languages of the arts – spirit, morality, service, chivalry, passion, stewardship. In the flat world, this is the language of philanthropy. The stories of Arthur's court that Cowie re-tells so engagingly remind us of the metaphorical blind spots that 'lean' language leaves in our corporate venues and, perhaps, as corporate language increasingly seeps into our larger public discourse, in our personal and civic lives as well.

*Human growth: left- and right-brain lenses.*

Cowie explores human development using both hemispheres of our brains. Through a left-brain lens she builds a carefully documented map of modern knowledge and thought about the human development process and how our growth journeys can be supported. Relying heavily on social science research, she describes the human development process as a series of growth phases. Each phase provides its own unique challenges, opportunities for trial and error, for support from others, and for lessons learned about universal growth themes. Each phase is a building block towards greater capability in more complex environments. Cowie reminds us that growth is a natural human drive, a process that, while not programmable, is largely understood, and can be shaped in part by the choices we make for ourselves and for our relationships with others.

It is significant that her work is grounded in human development research. We are too often distracted by the barrage of pop-science, self-help, get-ahead-quick, how-to-use-your-power, leadership-for-dummies advice purveyed in popular books and articles, and by gurus on speaking tours.

Using the right-brain lens of story, Cowie delightfully engages us in an exploration of the mysterious side of human development that is more the realm of spirit than science. In contrast to the lean language of the flat world, the language of mythology is three-dimensional – rich textures of imagery, emotion and human struggle.

The parallel narratives, which share similar themes, are helpful complements to each other. Hopefully, you will let your right and left hemispheres work together as you read through the text.

*Mythology as metaphor: enriching our growth stories.*

Joseph Campbell helped us recognise the value of mythology as an archive of peoples' collective, common experience. Mythology calls us into the long stream of human striving that extends well before and forever beyond our own lifetime. The stories are larger than, and yet common to, us. Mythological language is the metaphor of life experience before science, before precise measures, before industrialisation brought people together in factories – when life was local. It is also the language of ageless human capacity – good, evil, love, hate, spirit, courage, risk, jealousy, self-sacrifice, extraordinary heroism, and shame. We are reminded that these universal themes continue to be enacted in all of our individual life spaces – corporate, private and public. Mythology is a storyboard background that gives colour and life to our every-day flat-world language of numbers, efficiency, and performance. We are reminded that we can invest our lives in organisations for more than a paycheck.

Cowie uses the Arthurian legend to highlight the significance of the growth stories we are writing in each of our lives. The legend suggests to us the wonder, the magic, the glory, the excitement and the adventure in our own journeys. We are reminded not to take our Self for granted, as if we were a common commodity in the larger forces beyond our control. For, while a process common to all, each of our individual human development journeys is a quite extraordinary thing in its own right.

*Building holding environments for human development in organisations.*

Cowie introduces the concept of 'holding environments' as the containers for the work we do in growth phases. This is, itself, a powerful metaphor and particularly useful for organisational life in the flat world. Round-world methods for growing individuals in organisations, such as training, sabbaticals, and even mentor relationships, seem somehow too linear, too serial for fluid, contemporary organisations. Just-in-time supply chains, customer service demands, technology breakthroughs, uncertain employment, and speedy and constant change mitigate against traditionally programmed approaches to professional development. Individual development programs are treated as paper-driven formalities. Trainers are asked to shorten training programs to accommodate jammed participant schedules. When individuals do meet or train together, they do so in airport hotels to minimise travel time, or on-line, in virtual meeting rooms through

digitally mediated broadband. Constantly checking their smart-
phones, participants are rarely given time (or choose to take time)
to slow down, reflect on what has been learned and live in the
'A-ha' moments that are developmental growth spurts.

So, if we think they are important, we have to be concerned
about the holding environments for human development in the
flat world. Some learning mechanisms have evolved in large part
as adaptations to flat-world realities. Coaching has skyrocketed
as a professional development practice. It is flat-world-friendly
– focused solely on one client whose schedule can be accommo-
dated. It requires no travel by the client and can often be conducted by telephone. It is customised, targeted and focused.
Client time is not 'wasted' in the often messy and time-consuming
process of accommodating the learning needs of others. Another
emerging holding environment is action learning. As the name
suggests, teams learn while 'in action', together tackling a critical
need for their organisation. Rotational assignments are also used
as development mechanisms in many organisations, although
often not supported in ways that optimise their learning potential. In each of these examples, learning and professional development are brought 'on line' into the organisational work-flow.

Coaching and action learning are, indeed, useful adaptations to today's professional development needs. Cowie speaks to
coaching, in particular, in acknowledgement of its possibilities.
It is technical training, however, being most easily related to the
bottom line and critical to the successful implementation of technology, that continues to be a priority, though delivered in ever
increasingly efficient ways via multimedia.

Cowie invites us to consider whether these and similar mechanisms are sufficient for meeting the leadership and contributor
needs of the flat-world future. Given the higher-order stage of
human development her model describes, I believe we must continue to develop viable, productive learning approaches in today's
and tomorrow's organisations as elements of the new holding

environments she proposes, lest our human capabilities be out-distanced by the technological and economic forces of the flat world. Seemingly, the metaphorical language of these new holding environments will also need to be richer, more provocative, more nourishing than the lean language of flat-world business. The range and depth of personal and professional exploration evoked will need to be much broader and deeper than is provided by everyday life in business. What might this kind of holding space look like in organisations? How does an organisation provide this space for growth in a lean, speeded-up flat world? These are challenges going forward.

Cowie provides a development conceptual road map for organisations and individuals. She suggests practical, often powerful ways for individuals and organisations to work from her roadmap. Her map, her stories from myth and her practice suggestions remind us of the great potential that individuals bring to their work life, much of it untapped. She also reminds us of the significance of our work experience to our life's development journey and how we, if no one else, must take greater notice and control of the holding environments we choose or create.

*The ongoing adventure.*

And so, as in the mythological metaphor around which Cowie builds her book, we venture forth to meet the dragons of danger and opportunity as we make our way in the unfolding flat world. As it was with the questing knights, the development is in the journey. Let Cowie be a Merlin to you as you read her book.

TED TSCHUDY

# A Story for our Lifetime
## The Search for the Grail

❋

We know, from the anthropological record, that we have been telling stories to each other since the dawn of civilisation. When we harness the power of imagination and metaphor we are able to make sense of the world: seemingly disconnected things cohere; truths which were hidden are revealed; and answers to our questions become clear.

This is a book about the human development journey which has, of course, been the subject of the stories of every people, and of every time. As the author, I have drawn upon one such story, the legend of King Arthur and his Knights of the Round Table, to illustrate my interpretation of the journey. An ancient tale it may be, but it is also a story for *our* lifetime.

The Arthurian legend has its origins in the chronicles and poetry of the Dark Age Celts. It was popularised in the Middle Ages, a time when the Britons were a race without a recorded history, by the Welsh ecclesiastic, Geoffrey of Monmouth. His epic piece, *Historia Regum Britanniae* (circa 1136), spanned two millennia from the founding of Britain by Brutus to the coming of the Saxons in the seventh century of our era, and was read eagerly by those to whom Latin was available, and accepted as authoritative.

The story of the Dark Age King and his counsellor, Merlin, was then embellished with the vitality and colour of twelfth-century courtly life by the medieval French romancers. Their tales of the adventures of King Arthur's chivalric brotherhood were immediately translated, imitated (plagiarised) and augmented by writers across Europe and Scandinavia. Then, in 1469–70, the prisoner knight, Sir Thomas Malory, reworked the legend into its most familiar form, *Le Morte Darthur*, a masterpiece of honour and shame, of fidelity and betrayal, of good men and women and their fall.

The new world of the eighteenth century, a time of science and reason, was necessarily opposed to the marvel and mystery of medieval literature, whereupon the legend became, temporarily, a tradition in retreat. But it enjoyed a revival during the nineteenth century (as a reaction to the rational world-view of the Enlightenment) in the form of Alfred, Lord Tennyson's mystical *Idylls of the King*. And, in recent decades, it has become part of popular culture, or *real* folklore, through the media of the novel and cinematic film. Of the many Arthurian quests, it is, of course, the mysterious and haunting search for the Grail which is best known.

KATE COWIE
Aberdeenshire, Scotland
April 2012

# Acknowledgements

*

This book is written in my name and it is the product of seven years of reading and writing and many more of practice; but it is also the product of seven years of conversations that I have had with Ken Ideus, whom I feel privileged to call one of my greatest mentors.

Ken received his Doctorate in Education, specialising in management and corporate education, from Boston University. Grounded in the theory of human development, he is forged, too, by four decades of experience of helping people in organisations transform the way they exercise their leadership. I first met Ken in 2001 when I held the position of Organisation Development Manager in Royal Dutch Shell's UK Exploration and Production business. Ken was invited into Shell to introduce his pioneering thinking in the practice of executive coaching. Even then this was a populous field but Ken distinguished himself, as he continues to do now, with an extraordinary ability to help organisational leaders reframe their business challenges into opportunities for personal growth, opportunities to help others grow, and opportunities for the enterprise they lead to play a more meaningful role in our new, globalised world.

From very early in our acquaintance, Ken guided me in my reading and thinking. As he and I talked, I heard again names I was familiar with from my own postgraduate studies of a quarter of a century ago: Carl Jung, Jean Piaget, Abraham Maslow and Lawrence Kohlberg – names which will be familiar to many whatever their discipline or area of expertise. But I learned new names, too: names of other seminal researchers such as Jane Loevinger, Robert Kegan and the name, too, of Ken Wilber, one of the most important integral thinkers of our time. Ken Ideus is also an integral thinker. He weaves his knowledge of the different strands of developmental psychology into a philosophy of humanity – of who we are and who we could be – and from this position of possibility walks alongside those whom he coaches, guiding them forward, learning with them along the way.

Ken and I spoke of how difficult it is for those with whom we work – leaders in organisations who are, typically, busy beyond stretch, stewarding their enterprises into the future – to have this same precious chance: to dedicate time to learn about the business of being human, making sense of human experiences. And so the idea emerged to map the human development journey for them, to make accessible the discoveries of the modern theorists, enabling them, thereby, to identify opportunities for growth for themselves, for those whom they lead and also for their organisation. Ken had long been intrigued by the literary figure of the magician, Merlin – Counsellor to all the Dark Age Kings and Guide to those who seek the Grail – as a symbol of a masterful coach. I, meanwhile, as a former student of English language and literature at the University of Bristol, was equally fascinated with the knight errant quest as a medieval narrative device for depicting the human adventure. Soon we realised that we could use the story of the search for the Grail to organise all our thinking – our subject has, after all, been the study of all peoples since earliest times and, from those times, the image of a long, meandering pathway has been regularly and variously employed to represent it.

Ken Ideus is, therefore, very much a part of this book. His thinking has shaped it. Even the title, *Finding Merlin*, is his. For this reason, it is dedicated to him. It serves as a vessel for a measure of his wisdom from which anyone who reads it can draw.

I would like to extend my grateful thanks to Derek, James and Thomas Cowie, Sheila Lilley and Christeen Bell.

The illustrations in the book are by Rob Ward.

# FINDING MERLIN

## A HANDBOOK

*for the*

## HUMAN

## DEVELOPMENT

# JOURNEY

—◆— *IN OUR NEW* —◆—

## ORGANISATIONAL WORLD

# Introduction

*I. The universal quest.*

e are all on a Quest. Whoever we are, we are all searching for something – something that we have not yet found, something which is just out of reach, compelling us to extend our journey until we find it.

This is not a statement of some newly discovered truth. The motif of a long, meandering journey is a recurring and pervasive image in the cultural artefacts of all human societies. Labyrinth designs, for example, dating back thousands of years, appear on rock faces, coins, walls, pottery, mosaic pavements and manuscripts on every continent of the world.[1]

THE CLASSIC LABYRINTH *is also known as the Cretan labyrinth, so named because of its association with the mythical creature, the Minotaur of Crete, and with Cretan coins imprinted with the image minted in the fourth and fifth centuries* BCE.

*The ancient image of the labyrinth is always a single, meandering pathway which weaves and circles towards the centre. Some of the earliest examples yet recovered appear in Neolithic and Bronze Age rock carvings in Europe, North Africa and the American Southwest. The maze is a later image of the same journey. It is a multicursal route of wrong turns and dead ends, and the traveller must make many choices along the way, but still there is only one correct path to the central goal.*[2]

During the medieval period, the motif was employed extensively in the popular stories of King Arthur's Company of the Round Table. Against the backdrop of the order and bounty of the court, the Knights Errant ride out into the mysterious forest, following twisting, forking, circuitous pathways, where strange creatures, besieged castles and heroines in need of deliverance await. With the help of a guide, they overcome these extraordinary challenges in battles which test their chivalric worth. Periodically, they return to the court for feast times and tournaments — occasions for the public acknowledgement and celebration of their achievements thus far. And then they ride out again on what is a continuous search for adventures. Of the many Arthurian quests, it is the pursuit of "the thing that was called the Grail" which is best known.[3]

### II. A journey into oneself.

 hen we encounter a cross-cultural and enduring motif such as this, we can be sure that it has served those who have gone before us in that primary activity of being human — meaning-making, making sense of human experiences.[4] Scholars who have studied it in its many different forms have identified that its occurrence always signifies "a journey into oneself"[5]: it is the universal 'Search for Self', the search for who we are and, moreover, who we can be.[6]

This journey, which we undertake from infancy through to late adulthood (and some would say beyond that), is often called the 'growth of consciousness'. The road we follow as we make this journey is represented in the Arthurian legend as the long, meandering path which each knight rides as he quests to prove himself. It was first charted in earnest by the early philosophers and mystics who came forward from 1600 BCE. They described it as one of many sequential stages — stages of self-identity and self-growth — each of which we must attain and incorporate into our sense of who we are if we are to progress onwards.† Modern, orthodox researchers in different fields of human knowledge (in neuroanatomy, developmental psychology, anthropology and epistemology, for example) have also studied the question of how our development unfolds and, as one of the greatest integral thinkers of our time, Ken Wilber, notes,[7] the extraordinary fact is that they have all reached conclusions which are broadly aligned with the work of those first truth-seekers. They have also identified the 'journey into oneself' as a universal and cross-cultural experience of multiple stages of self-growth. And, with their refinements and enhancements, they have drawn their own different but related maps of it. In Chapter One, The Path Through the Forest, I offer a simplified account of the combined findings of these modern theorists.

The sobering news for the traveller, however, is that, despite the abundance of diagrams and charts, the quest for self-development is not an easy one: in the course of their strange, arduous and interwoven adventures, the Knights Errant become "*slowly wise*".[8] The pathway, itself, is difficult, *and* each stage of the journey provides its own set of challenges – intellectual, social, moral, emotional, psychological and even spiritual challenges – represented by the never-ending supply of giants and dragons and damsels in distress of the Arthurian world. These we must overcome and also incorporate into our sense of who we are, if we are to move on to the next stage of our development as a *fully integrated Self*. The social psychologist, Edgar Schein, refers to these chal-

---

† *The great 'Axial' sages (a term coined by the philosopher, Karl Jaspers) emerged circa 1600 BCE in societies torn apart by violence and warfare. "When they started to look for causes of violence in the psyche, the Axial philosophers penetrated their interior world and began to explore a hitherto undiscovered realm of human experience." They were succeeded between 800 and 300 BCE by, amongst others, Buddha, Socrates, Confucius and Jeremiah. These were a disparate group of thinkers and yet they shared similar ideas about the nature of humanity, teaching people "to seek the ideal, archetypal self within".[9]*

lenges as "issues to be confronted", which we address by engaging in "specific tasks".[10] If, in our determination to press ahead, we choose not to confront them, we will arrive at our next destination with some of our potential unrealised, with an imbalance in our sphere of total capability. And the further we travel along the pathway of growth, the greater the risk is of such developmental gaps appearing. Chapter Two, Giants and Dragons, describes these challenges in more detail, and the subsequent chapter, The Knight Adventurous, addresses the question of how our personality may influence the particular approach we take to conquer them.

### III. The road less travelled.

o, whilst the drive for self-development is innate and compelling, the journey is difficult. The early sages and modern theorists agree that its most distant reaches are available to all of us (barring organic or functional incapacity which can impose restrictions) but few of us ever achieve them. And in the search for the Grail, of course, it is only the greatest of knights who succeed.[11] It has, therefore, been described by the psychologist, Scott Peck, as the "road less travelled", marked by "legitimate suffering", and requiring courage and wisdom from those who do travel onwards.[12] The leadership scholar, Robert Quinn, using the language of the sixteenth-century contemplative, St John of the Cross, describes this experience similarly as "walking naked into the land of uncertainty... a terrifying choice, often involving a dark night of the soul".[13]

Happily, however, we need not travel alone. The mythologist, Joseph Campbell, has demonstrated that, in the stories of the 'Hero's Journey' which are found in the narrative record of every culture, the hero always has a helper.[14] In the Arthuriad, it is, of course, the magician, Merlin, Counsellor to all the Dark Age Kings and Guide of the Grail quest, who serves this purpose.

Ironically, however, in today's societies and in Western societies in particular, we are often reluctant to turn to others for help when we face challenging situations. We promote the individual work ethic over and above the group work ethic and, accordingly, honour and value self-reliance and personal achievement. So the social scientist, Chris Argyris, notes that well-educated, high-powered, highly committed professionals who occupy key leadership positions in the modern corporation prefer to be "productive loners"[15]; and so also the leadership scholar, Warren Bennis, and his co-author, Patricia Ward Biederman, observe that today's mythology only reinforces that preference:

"We cling to the myth of the Lone Ranger, the romantic idea that great things are usually accomplished by a larger-than-life individual working alone."[16]

But as Bennis and Ward Biederman also insist, "one is too small a number to produce greatness.... It's not clear that life was ever so simple that individuals, acting alone, solved most significant problems".[17] The fourth chapter of this book, A Magician for a Guide, explores, therefore, the role of helpers in our modern lives – people who have already encountered the challenges that we face now, and who can share their insights to help us overcome them. The chapter also includes a set of questions and suggestions for self-reflection. They are intended to help readers discover how far they have already travelled along their own development pathway, and what they need to do to press onwards (in terms of identifying the issues they need to confront and, importantly, the guides who can help them in their endeavour).

The fifth chapter, The Forest of Adventure, describes the role that our environment plays in our development. The forest surrounding Camelot provides exactly the right milieu for the questing knights, supplying them with food, shelter and a myriad of helpful hermits, as well as the now familiar stock of wrathful villains and fearsome beasts to test their worth. Today, most of us spend most of our waking hours in an organisation of one sort or another and, in favourable circumstances, this organisation functions as the 'culturing context' we need for our growth. But if we are not so fortunate – if it transpires that our working environment is not providing us with the stimulation we need – our responsibility to ourselves is to seek an alternative place of work, one which will foster (rather than hold in abeyance or, worse, stymie) our ongoing growth. The responsibility, meanwhile, of chief executives, organisational leaders, boards of directors, organisation development practitioners, human resource professionals, learning and development specialists, and talent and capability managers is to ensure that they offer an appropriate culturing context for all those who work in the organisations they steward. As a number of scholars have asserted, the relationship between the development of an individual and the development of an organisation is an interdependent one. To that end, the Conclusion explores the nature of this relationship, and lists some practical suggestions to help those charged with 'keeping the forest' create the conditions which will allow both people and their organisations to develop to their fullest potential.

### IV. The call to action.

y main purpose in writing this book is to provide a map of the human adventure, to make the knowledge of the early sages and modern theorists accessible to readers living and working in the 'real' world of today, enabling them, thereby, to extend their own learning journeys. The proverbial wisdom that old dogs cannot learn new tricks, and that leopards cannot change their spots, no longer holds true for *homo sapiens* (so aptly named 'thinking man'). Research has now demonstrated conclusively that neurogenesis (the capacity to generate new neurons) does occur in the mature human brain. We, as adult humans, can continue to learn beyond the first decades of our lives – *if we choose to*. Four short lines from Alfred, Lord Tennyson's *Ulysses* describe

this continuous journey of discovery which is available to us:

"I am a part of all that I have met;

Yet all experience is an arch wherethro'

Gleams that untravell'd world, whose margin fades

For ever and for ever when I move."[18]

And if we decline this opportunity? If we chose to remain at the point where we are now? (After all, we all know people who have stopped learning, and very comfortable they seem to be.) I borrow the oft-quoted words of Walter Pater, an influential thinker in the Aesthetic movement of the late nineteenth century, to illustrate the choice which is before us:

"A counted number of pulses only is given to us of a variegated, dramatic life. How may we see in them all that is to be seen in them by the finest senses? How shall we pass most swiftly from point to point, and be present always at the focus where the greatest number of vital forces unite in their purest energy?

"To burn always with this hard, gem-like flame, to maintain this ecstasy, is success in life. In a sense it might even be said that our failure is to form habits... [i.e.] on this short day of frost and sun, to sleep before evening."[19]

So, how may we ensure that we do not, in Pater's evocative words, "sleep before evening"? That endeavour *is* the universal quest – and the subject of this book.

# FINDING
# MERLIN

## *CHAPTER ONE*

# THE PATH
## *THROUGH*
# THE FOREST

*The Grail was created and
recreated by different writers throughout the
medieval period but, whether it is a jewel-encrusted
dish, a chalice or a wonder-making stone, it
always represents something beyond
the ordinary, and offers the
possibility of perfection
to those who seek
and find it.*[1]

✤ ✤
✤

# · CHAPTER ONE ·
# The Path Through the Forest

*I. The growth of consciousness: the growth of you.*

hilosophers through the ages from both the East and the West have asserted that we are all embarked upon a journey. It is a "journey into oneself"[2] which we experience, from infancy onwards, as an innate and compelling drive to discover who we are and, moreover, who we can be. This universal 'Search for Self' is often represented as a long, meandering pathway, an image that we find in the cultural artefacts of every human society.

During the medieval period, the knight errant quest was the dominant narrative device used to depict the journey.[3] In these stories the hero rides out into the forest following twisting, forking, circuitous trails which offer opportunities aplenty for false starts, wrong turns and dead ends. As he progresses, he achieves greater and greater levels of awareness which arise from the dynamic integration of the many different developmental experiences that he encounters.

One of the most important of the knight errant quests is Wolfram von Eschenbach's Middle High German masterpiece, *Parzival* (dated by literary scholars between 1200 and 1212).[4] So popular was this medieval German epic, it has survived in over seventy manuscripts. Its hero is Parzival, son of a great soldier-knight and a widowed queen, and his tale, told in no fewer than 24,810 lines and sixteen books, is the record of his many interweaving adventures (and misadventures) as he quests first for knighthood, then for opportunities to prove his knightly valour and, finally, for the mystifying and illusive "thing that was called the Grail". The story, retold briefly on the following pages is, demonstrably, a psychological allegory: the action turns not so much on the search for the Grail, but on the objective for which the search is undertaken. As Parzival rides away from his mother's house, he is an innocent making his entrance into the world; his ongoing quest represents his inner struggle to become "slowly wise".[5]

The first mystics mapped the human development road as a sequence of five developmental stages of increasing wholeness, ascending from matter to life, to mind, to soul and ultimately to spirit. Each dimension incorporates the components of its predecessor, and constitutes a new, higher – or more complex, more integrated, more differentiated – organisation. This holarchy of developmental stages is captured in the medieval concept of the *Scala Naturae* or the 'Great Chain of Being'.[6] It is often illustrated as a nest of concentric spheres, and forms the core of all the world's wisdom traditions.

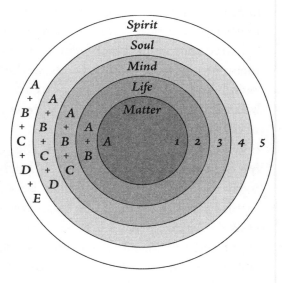

THE GREAT CHAIN OF BEING *The early mystics mapped five, sequential development stages of increasing wholeness.[7] Each dimension transcends and includes its predecessor, and so constitutes a new, higher order of being. If physical and physiochemical matter is favourable, life emerges; if life is favourable, mind emerges; if mind is favourable, soul (a level of awareness which transcends a body-bound entity) emerges; and if soul is favourable, spirit emerges which transcends all and which Wilber describes as "an ultimate oneness with the All, with the Kosmos".[8] The general principle of holism was articulated by the classical philosopher, Aristotle, in* The Metaphysics *thus: "The whole is more than the sum of the parts." The term 'holism' was coined by the statesman and philosopher, Jan Smuts, in his book,* Holism and Evolution *(1926).*

## Parzival's search for the Grail.[9]

arzival is introduced to us as a naïve youth, living an idyllic but sheltered life in the forest. He is cosseted by his mother, who has lost her husband through his pursuit of knightly glory and who, therefore, tries to isolate him from the world of courtly life and knighthood. But, one day, as he is hunting in the forest, he encounters three fine knights of King Arthur's Company. He is immediately captivated by them and determines to become one of them. His distraught mother dresses him in fool's clothes in the hope that mockery will drive him home, but, at the same time, offers him good advice on how to conduct himself (which he fails to understand, as his subsequent experiences demonstrate). Parzival then rides out in search of King Arthur to request that he be knighted, whereupon his mother dies of grief.

Events do not unfold well for Parzival. He finds a lady alone in a tent, steals kisses, a ring, a brooch and food from her, and then leaves her to face the retribution of her jealous husband. Next, he meets his cousin, Sigune (who will, through the course of the story, be a great source of help to him), weeping over the body of her slain suitor. Parzival is anxious to avenge this death but Sigune misdirects him in his pursuit of the murderer, believing that he will be hurt if he confronts him.

So Parzival rides on and reaches the court where he immediately demands of the King that he be knighted. The King replies that he will give him this honour and a suit of fine armour the following day. But Parzival will not wait and, instead, he races away to challenge the formidable Red Knight, whom he encountered on his approach to the court and whose magnificent red armour he covets.

By chance, he succeeds in slaying the Red Knight. A page helps him into his newly won, unfamiliar attire, and he rides out again. He reaches the castle of a kindly nobleman, Gurnemanz, who educates him in knightly ways for two weeks. Impatient for battle, he then departs for his next adventure – the deliverance of the besieged city of Belrepaire. Having defeated the hostile army, he marries the city's beautiful queen (although, still naïve, they both remain innocent for two nights). But, soon he is eager for more adventures.

He rides out yet again and discovers the rich Fisher King, moored in his boat on a lake, and accepts his invitation to lodge at his castle for the night. The Fisher King is wounded and can only be released from his suffering by the one who is destined to win the Grail and ask the question: "Sire, what ails you?" That night, Parzival witnesses a wondrous ceremony in which "a thing that was called the Grail, earth's perfection's transcendence" is carried into the hall where the company is seated for dinner. Parzival feasts with them, served by the Grail with whatever food or drink he desires, and receives from the Fisher King a precious sword which, his host explains, he used in many battles before his body was crippled. But Parzival, misinterpreting Gurnemanz's advice not to ask too many questions, fails to release the Fisher King from his agony.

He departs the following morning, leaving behind what seems to be an empty castle. Only a page appears, to lower the drawbridge and shout words of angry disappointment as Parzival rides away into the forest. There he meets Signue for a second time, and she also reproaches him for not relieving the Fisher King. More adventures ensue for Parzival until he rejoins King Arthur and his knights at the court. He is welcomed joyfully and commended for the great honour he has brought to the King and the Round Table through his victorious exploits, but his delight at this reception is short-lived for, suddenly, the ugly sorceress, Cundrie, breaks in upon the revelry and curses him in front of all those gathered there for his lack of compassion for the Fisher King's plight.

Smarting from this public humiliation, and rejecting God in injured pride for allowing this to happen, Parzival rides out again to find the Grail. For more than four years he wanders in despondent knight-errantry until he rediscovers his cousin, now a recluse. She withdraws her earlier reproaches, and advises him to follow the tracks of the recently departed Cundrie, who knows the way to the Grail Castle. But Parzival fails to find her. More adventures befall him until he encounters a group of pilgrims on Good Friday[†], who remind him that it was on this day that God proved his love for mankind.

In chastened mood, he meets his hermit uncle, who also instructs him in the meaning of the Passion[*]; on hearing this, Parzival casts off his pride and becomes reconciled to God. His uncle then explains to him the mysteries of the Grail, and charges him with the three sins of causing the death of his mother (of which Parzival was unaware until now), of slaying the Red Knight (who, it transpires, was a near kinsman), and of failing to ask the compassionate question to relieve the Fisher King. The hermit then absolves Parzival of his sins, and he rides out yet again in search of the Grail.

With more successful adventures to his credit, he returns to Arthur's court, where Cundrie reappears to proclaim him 'Lord of the Grail', and guide him to the Grail Castle. Once there, Parzival asks the redeeming question and relieves the Fisher King of his agony. Order is restored in the land, the Fisher King yields his place as ruler of the Grail community to Parzival, and the hero is then reunited with his queen. ✤

† Good Friday is the day in the Christian calendar when adherents remember the crucifixion of Christ.
* The 'Passion' is the Gospel narrative of the sufferings of Christ on the Cross.

Many modern, orthodox researchers in the field of psychology have also studied the question of how our development unfolds, and their findings confirm the insights of the ancients. Universally and cross-culturally, consciousness (or awareness) emerges in a sequence of distinct stages of self-identity and self-growth, each of which we must attain and incorporate into our sense of who we are if we are to progress to the next one without compromise.†
The theorists are also in agreement with the philosophers about the means by which consciousness emerges: it is by the agency of two fundamental capacities, *transcendence* and *inclusion*. Initially, we identify or fuse with a stage of development but, over time, we discover that the strengths of this stage are, ultimately, its limitations, and so we work to differentiate ourselves from it and then to incorporate it into our sense of Self, before moving on, if growth continues, to identify with a new, higher stage of development.

† *As the Arthurian scholar, Otto Springer, explains, the experiences of Parzival do not take an accidental course; they represent the successive phases of the hero's inner metamorphoses.*[10] *His achievement of each phase is marked during his periodic visits to the court where he is feted for the honour he has brought to the King and to the Round Table through his many conquests. When his struggle is complete, of course, he ascends to the throne of the Kingdom of the Grail.*

## II. A map for the journey.

o the pathway along which we are all travelling has been a subject of contemplation and study for millennia. In this chapter, I draw on the work of modern researchers, including, in particular, that of the pre-eminent developmental psychologist, Robert Kegan (who, in turn, drew on the pioneering work of the epistemologist, Jean Piaget) to provide a simplified map of the human adventure. It is a map which charts the seven most commonly experienced stages of the development road – stages of self-identity and self-growth – which we navigate by the mechanisms of transcendence and inclusion described above. Our journey begins in infancy at the Sensorimotor stage. Then follow the Impulsive stage of early childhood, the Imperial stage of late childhood, the Relational stage of adolescence, and the Organisational stage of young adulthood, all of which most of us achieve. Only a small percentage of us achieve the subsequent World-Centric stage; and the highest position, the Self-Transcendent stage (the realm of those frontier sages and mystics), is a very rare accomplishment indeed.

*Self-Transcendent stage*

*World-Centric stage*

*Organisational stage*

*Relational stage*

*Imperial stage*

THE HUMAN ADVENTURE
*The individual first identifies or fuses*

*Impulsive stage*

*with a stage of development, but, over time, discovers that the strengths of that stage are, ultimately, its limitations, and so works to differentiate himself from it and then incorporate it into his sense of Self, before moving on, if growth continues, to identify with a new, higher stage of development.*

*Sensorimotor stage*

- *Sensorimotor stage*  In the first few months of my life I cannot differentiate myself from the physical world: I am, essentially, a sensorimotor organism.
- *Impulsive stage*  I am a young child now, and a separate Self with purposes of my own which I seek to fulfil. I have my own perceptions, too; and, as I cannot distinguish yet between how something appears to me and how something *is*, my life is filled with fantasy.

+ *Imperial stage* As an older child, I have a self-concept and I become invested in that sense of Self through personal aggrandisement, display and competition. My care and concern extend to my group – but no further!

+ *Relational stage* As an adolescent, I learn that others have needs, too, and so I become empathetic and invested in my relationships. I seek inclusion, affiliation and nurturance.

+ *Organisational stage* As a young adult, I desire independence. My concern is to preserve a new-found autonomy, and to seek group recognition of it through organisational involvement.

+ *World-Centric stage* At last I can embrace a truly global perspective: my group is not the only group in the universe!

+ *Self-Transcendent stage* I have now achieved a depth of consciousness which is not confined to my individual Self.

But, before we explore this development pathway, let us pause to understand how the brain matures through the life cycle, because repeated studies have demonstrated that our biological and mental functioning are interrelated.

### III. The development of the brain through the life cycle.

 ost of the brain's one hundred billion neurons are formed and then migrate to their assigned positions during embryonic and early postnatal life. The brain of a newborn child, however, is only one-quarter to one-third of its adult volume; it continues to grow postnatally according to a genetically determined programme of *overproduction* of axons, dendrites and synapses.

This exuberant increase in brain connections is complemented, from the age of four months onwards, by a concurrent process of dendritic pruning and synapse elimination which is driven by environmental influences.[11] Those synaptic connections which are activated by experience survive and strengthen ("neurons that fire together wire together"[12]), and those which are not utilised gradually disappear through lack of use, so that, over time, a more efficient set of neural connections is created. Experience, therefore, plays a necessary, organising role in the development of the brain's structure and, as we shall discover in this and the next chapter, it serves as an essential catalyst for the development of the mind, too. As our neural circuitry becomes increasingly specialised, and as we experience events which do not conform to our existing beliefs, we are nudged to reinterpret those events, to react to them in new ways, and so achieve more and more sophisticated levels of functional maturity.[13] The human mind, in sum, emerges from the interaction of the brain *with* experience.

These special sequences of progressive cell proliferation and regressive synapse elimination described above unfold until the third decade of life. Thereafter, more conscious effort is required of us if our minds are to continue to develop. Contrary to previously held assumptions, recent research has now demonstrated that neurogenesis (the capacity to generate new neurons) does

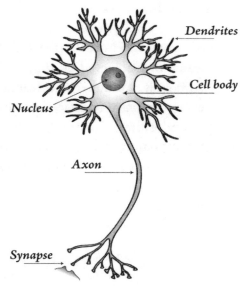

NEURONS *are the building blocks of the brain. An axon is the long, slender projection of a neuron which conducts electrical impulses away from the neuron's cell body. Axons are the primary transmission lines of the brain. Dendrites are the branched projections of a neuron which conduct the electrochemical stimulation received from other neurons to the cell body of the neuron from which they project. An axon 'connects' with a dendrite at a synapse – a gap which is bridged by chemicals called neurotransmitters (transmitter substances) which are contained in the terminal buttons of the sending neuron. When these neurotransmitters are electrically stimulated by the axon, they are released across the synaptic cleft onto specialised receptor sites in the receiving dendrite of the next neuron in the neural net.*[14]

occur in the mature human brain.† Animal studies, meanwhile, have revealed the important role that an enriched environment plays in fostering this process. Stimulation increases the number of new neurons and the density of synaptic connections in the hippocampus (a region of the brain important for learning and memory). It also enhances their rate of survival.[15] From this, we may conclude that we, as adult humans, can continue to learn beyond the first decades of our lives, but we must choose to do so actively by seeking a stimulating context in which to live and work.

Over time, however, as the developmental psychologist, Ian Stuart-Hamilton, explains, the balance between *plasticity* (or the capacity for change) and *stability* becomes progressively weighted towards the latter, and neuroimaging techniques reveal a precipitous decline in brain density (through the loss of axonal fibres and neuronal shrinkage) in the later decades of life. Research by gerontologists consistently shows a corresponding decline in cognitive abilities in eighty-five to ninety per cent of the population during these decades, too. For many, this decline is considerable, with the elderly achieving mean scores in cognitive tests which are, on average, nearly two standard deviations lower than the mean scores achieved by young adults.[16]

Happily, a number of researchers have found that neural and, hence, cognitive functioning can be improved in old age with physical exercise: neural health depends upon the efficient flow of oxygenated blood to the brain which physical exercise promotes. Other researchers have identified that mental stimulation (which also increases cerebral blood flow) has positive effects in the elderly, too. If, therefore, we want to stave off what would otherwise be near-certain cognitive decline in old age in order that

---

† *"Do you remember being told that you were born with a finite number of brain cells and that, from the moment you were born, these were dying away, never to be replaced? It's a common misconception... the brain is not something formed during the first twenty years of our lives and in a state of decay ever after. It is a moving, changing, fluid organ that interacts with its environment."*[17] – Robert Winston

our minds may continue to develop, maintaining a physical and mental exercise regime is likely to be beneficial.

Equipped now with a basic understanding of neuroanatomy and the neurological changes which occur through the life cycle, we are ready to explore the development pathway available to us. We begin where every human adventure begins, in the first weeks after our birth.

*IV. The stages of the human development road.*

> KNOWLEDGE IS A FUNCTION OF BEING. WHEN THERE IS A CHANGE IN THE BEING OF THE KNOWER, THERE IS A CORRESPONDING CHANGE IN THE NATURE AND AMOUNT OF KNOWING.[18]
> · ALDOUS HUXLEY ·

*IV. a. The growth and loss of the Sensorimotor stage.*

 uring the period of my early infancy, I am essentially a sensorimotor organism: I am so identified with the physical world (particularly with my primary carers) that I cannot distinguish between the world and myself. As Kegan explains:

"As a newborn I live in a completely undifferentiated world, one in which nothing is on the side of object, in which nothing is other than me, in which everything I sense is taken to be an extension of me, and where anything ceases even to *be* once it is out of my sight, touch, hearing."[19]

I am wholly egocentric, meaning not that I think selfishly about myself, but, on the contrary, that I am *incapable* of thinking about myself, because to do so would require an ability to experience myself as separate from my environment. But, at around four months old, I begin to differentiate between sensations in my body and my external surroundings, and so the *physical* Self is born, a process which is completed by the time I am ten months old. By now, I have also achieved the foundational awareness of object permanency – the knowledge that an object can continue to exist even when it is no longer visible:

"The interest of a child of four or five months can be recruited to a colourful object or crinkly piece of cellophane. But if the object is covered, the child acts as if it no longer exists. Somewhere around eight to ten months most children begin to act differently. They reach out with their little fingers and pull away whatever conceals the object. The object is somehow 'there' in the world of the infant in a way it simply was not before."[20]

Crawling, perhaps walking, I move from one such object to another, grasping and exploring: there is a world separate from me, and 'I' am something other. 'I' am that which co-ordinates my reflexes, movements and sensations (which previously were only occurring outside me). The realisation that I am a separate Self existing in a separate world may be marked by the often misunderstood 'Terrible Twos' but, as Kegan explains, my negativism and wilfulness are simply an expression of normal growth, a declaration of my newly found distinctness, my sense *that* I am.[21] It is a repudiation of my former, undifferentiated Self (so I am learning to say 'no' to *that*) rather than a repudiation of my parents whom I will continue to return to for the safety and security they provide for many years yet.[22]

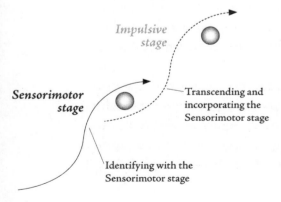

Impulsive stage

Sensorimotor stage

Transcending and incorporating the Sensorimotor stage

Identifying with the Sensorimotor stage

SUMMARY *So the sensorimotor infant first* identifies *with the physical world (becomes fused with it), then* transcends *it by folding into herself her reflexes, movements and sensations (so that she has* them rather than *is them), and then* incorporates *them into her sense of Self as she discovers that she is a separate Self. If her growth continues, she will move on to identify with a new, higher stage of development: the Impulsive stage.*

*IV. b. The growth and loss of the Impulsive stage.*

s a separate Self, I now have purposes and inten-
tions in which I am immersed and which I am,
therefore, driven to fulfil. I do not sit still for any
length of time; I have a short attention span for
anything involving the accommodation of others;
and I fill my language with 'me' and 'mine', as I busy myself with
claiming my world.

I am also embedded in my perceptions: I cannot distinguish
between the subjective appearance of things and 'reality' – how
something appears to me and how something *is*. A narcissistic or
'magical' atmosphere, therefore, characterises this stage. In the
words of Kegan, my life is filled with fantasy, and fantasy about
the fantastic[23]:

"The typical four-year-old child has a host of original and (to
our minds) amusingly strange views about nature. She may believe
the moon follows people when they walk; and if you and she walk
off in different directions it can follow both of you with no feeling on the child's part of any contradiction. Or he may believe it
is possible one day to become older than his older brother, so that
he can mete out the same kind of oppression his older brother is
now visiting upon him."[24]

But, gradually, between the ages of five and seven, a capacity
to conceptualise emerges and I begin to distinguish between how
something appears to me and how it really is. With this capacity, a self-concept develops, a more or less consistent, albeit sim-
plistic, notion of a 'me' (*what* I am as opposed to my earlier sense
of Self, *that* I am), and so I am now able to separate myself from
my impulses. At the same time, those around me are holding me
responsible for regulating them and, as I become more confident
of my ability to do so, I assume a new authority for myself (which,
before, had to be exercised by others). I become, in Kegan's words,
a child who is "in business for itself".[25] An important point to

note here is that, as my capacity to conceptualise unfolds, I not only recognise myself as a distinct person, I recognise 'the other' as such, too – someone with purposes and perceptions of their own. For the first time, I can *take the role of 'the other'* – a paradigm shift in my awareness which marks my emergence from the ego-centric stance of infancy to a socio-centric stance, enabling me to begin the process of accommodating others.

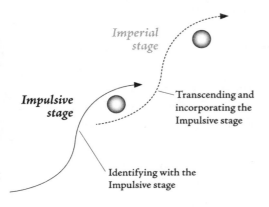

*Imperial stage*

*Impulsive stage*

Transcending and incorporating the Impulsive stage

Identifying with the Impulsive stage

SUMMARY *So the impulsive child first identifies with her impulses (becomes fused with them), then transcends them by folding them into herself, and then incorporates them into her sense of Self (so that she has them rather than is them), as an authority for herself emerges. If her growth continues, she will move on to identify with a new, higher stage of development: the Imperial stage.*

## IV. c. The growth and loss of the Imperial stage.

ith an awareness of *what* I am, and with a sense, too, of agency, power and freedom, I become invested in myself, and in meeting, therefore, my own needs, interests and wishes. The behavioural hallmarks of my new maturity are self-aggrandisement and display as I affirm my just-discovered, self-centred, self-asserting and self-determining concept of 'me':

"…in its fullest flush of confidence this is the bike-riding, money-managing, card-trading, wristwatch-wearing, pack-running, code-cracking, coin-collecting, self-waking, puzzle-solving nine-or-ten-year-old known to us all."[26]

Peer associations, facilitated by my emerging socio-centric stance, are an important venue for this affirmation process. These groups, as the psychologist, Kevin Durkin, explains, are made up of people who are 'similar' to me. We have the same developmental needs and, importantly, we are drawn from the same family backgrounds – we come from the same neighbourhood, the same social class, we share the same ethnicity and we speak the same language – and others are easily ostracised.[27] My socio-centrism is, therefore, ethnocentric: my care and concern have extended from myself to my group – but no further! (And in recent years, of course, psychologists and education specialists have succeeded in focusing the attention of politicians on this alienating behaviour, with the consequence that anti-bullying measures are featuring on many governments' agendas for schools.) As Kegan explains, an important aspect of these primary-school cultures is that they are regularised by rules and rituals which provide a framework for their members' display; he supplies a vivid example of this characteristic, the clubhouse conventions of a gang of ten-year-old girls (which also illustrate the ostracism of age mates who are not part of the club)[†]:

+ Do not tell a white lie unless necessary.
+ Do not hit anyone, except Ronny.
+ Do not use words worse than 'brat'.
+ Do not make faces, except at Ronny.
+ Do not make a hog or pig of yourself.
+ Do not tattle, except on Ronny.
+ Do not steal, except from Ronny.
+ Do not be a sneak.
+ Do not destroy other people's property, except Ronny's.
+ Do not be grumpy, except at Ronny.[28]

† *In Chapter Two, six streams of development are described – the Intellectual, Social, Moral, Emotional, Psychological and Spiritual streams – which flow through the basic stages of development described in this chapter. In the above list of clubhouse rules, we find an indication not just of the stage of development that the girls have reached (the Imperial stage) but also of their progression along the Social and Moral streams, too. "It's OK to pick on Ronny because Ronny is not a member of our gang" might be their rationale.*

But, gradually, as I approach adolescence, I sense that my imperial way of organising my world is not working: my family, teachers and friends make me aware that my self-centred behaviour is no longer tolerable. Now I am required to take the feelings of others into account, to keep commitments, and to meet expectations; and so a new Self emerges which is able to co-ordinate my concerns with the concerns of others, and to construct, for the first time, interpersonal relationships.

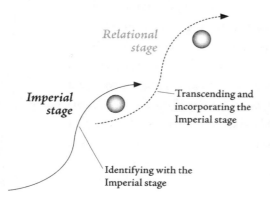

SUMMARY *So the imperial child first identifies* with her needs, interests and wishes (becomes fused with them), then transcends *them by folding them into herself, and then* incorporates *them into her sense of Self (so that she* has *them rather than* is *them) as an awareness of the concerns of others emerges. If her growth continues, she will move on to identify with a new, higher stage of development: the Relational stage.*

## IV. d. The growth and loss of the Relational stage.

ith the realisation that others have needs, I become empathetic and orientated towards mutuality. I am invested in my relationships, indeed, I *am* my relationships. At my former stage of development, I constructed my interactions with others, at least in part, for the purposes of self-aggrandisement and display. Now I construct them to support my new desire for inclusion, affiliation and nurturance. As Kegan explains:

"You are the other by whom I complete myself, the other whom I need to create the context out of which I define and know myself and the world."[29]

Within these relationships I am the giver as well as the receiver of care as I organise myself around the concerns of 'the other'.

Thousands, if not millions, of teenage love songs – songs of 'together forever' and songs of broken hearts – have been sold into this market of newly found 'otherness', fuelled, of course, by bio-systems awash with hormones. My socio-centric world-view (which was beginning to unfold as I emerged from the Impulsive stage) is now firmly established.

But, gradually, I can expect a conflict to arise within me between a desire to love and be loved, versus a desire for independence. Typically, those around me will also begin to demand that I assume responsibility for my own initiatives and preferences. I develop a point of view – about politics, books, sport, religion – in my discussions with my philosophical contemporaries. I begin to make decisions *for myself*, I engage in activities *for me*, and I look ahead to the adventure of leaving my parental home with a sense of excitement and freedom. Kegan captures this transition with the question: "Who is in charge around here, anyway?"[30] A new Self is unfolding which favours the themes of self-ownership, self-regulation and self-dependency.

But note that some chronologically aged adults do not emerge from the Relational stage to achieve autonomy, either because they do not choose to do so, or because the support they need from others to grow is not available.† (Such support includes recognising them as independent people, admitting them to an adult group or a societal arena, publicly recognising their achievements, and facilitating their entry into the world of work.[31]) And the consequences for those individuals of being, in Kegan's words, chronologically adult but psychologically adolescent can be devastating:

---

† *In Chapter Five, we explore the potential liabilities for a person of an inadequate development environment at each stage of their journey. In this chapter, however, we focus on the* typical *growth experience of individuals. Most people achieve the Relational stage, and most of those who do will then move on to achieve the Organisational stage. Only a small percentage of the population reaches the World-Centric stage; the Self-Transcendent stage is an even rarer accomplishment.*

"When I live in this balance as an adult I am the prime candidate for the assertiveness trainer, who may tell me that I need to learn how to stand up for myself, be more 'selfish', less pliable, and so on, as if these were mere skills to be added on to whoever else I am. The popular literature will talk about me as lacking self-esteem, or as a pushover because I want other people to like me. But this does not quite address me in my predicament, or in my 'hoping'. It is more that there *is* no self independent of the context of 'other people liking'."[32]

Fortunately, however, the majority of us do emerge from the Relational stage to achieve the next stage of development: the Organisational stage.

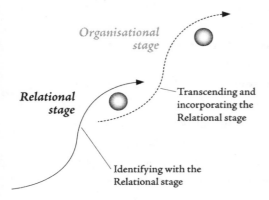

*Organisational stage*

*Relational stage*

Transcending and incorporating the Relational stage

Identifying with the Relational stage

SUMMARY *So the relational adolescent first* identifies *with her relationships (becomes fused with them), then* transcends *them by folding them into herself, and then* incorporates *them into her sense of Self (so that she* has *them rather than* is *them) as an independent selfhood emerges. If her growth continues, she will move on to identify with a new, higher stage of development: the Organisational stage.*

## IV. e. The growth and loss of the Organisational stage.

ith an independent selfhood, I have, for the first time, an awareness of *who* I am, and my strength is, in Kegan's words, my capacity to sustain myself, to parent myself, to name myself.[33] Typically, I will now seek group recognition of my selfhood through organisational involvement. As Durkin explains:

"...societies often arrange things so that one of the principal routes to autonomy is... getting a job."[34]

An organisation with an ideology which aligns with the personal philosophy I have been formulating (consciously or otherwise) throughout my adolescence will be very appealing to me, enabling me to translate my beliefs into actions in the world.[35] And the structured and regularised context of an established organisational setting will also be ideally suited to supporting me at this stage of my development because it will foster me in my exercises of self-discipline, personal achievement, pride in myself and ambition. In such an environment, I can find my own place; build networks of colleagues who can help me when I need them to do so; demonstrate and define myself through my activities; and satisfy my desire for progression, status and financial reward. Here I can fully immerse myself: it is the place in which I am able to be the person I have *become*.

But, as with all the foregoing evolutionary stages, the distinguishing characteristic of the Organisational stage (its self-possession) is also its limitation – and one which tends to manifest itself more clearly in the private arenas of friendship and love than in the public arena of work and career. 'Others', who were so important to me at the Relational stage, are not lost, but at the Organisational stage I know them differently – as being in service of my autonomous identity – and, whilst my closest adult relationships may be mutually supportive, warm and loving, they will not be intimate.[36] Over time, therefore, I may experience a growing sense of loneliness, even isolation in my relationships as they are currently constructed, which may be reinforced by those with whom I have them beginning to demand that I grant them their own individuality, their distinctness from the maintenance of my self-system.[37] If I am to emerge from this developmental stage, I will need to learn to place my independent Self in the bigger context of *inter*dependence, so that genuinely adult, intimate relationships become possible. In so doing, I will scrutinise the socio-centric or ethnocentric perspectives in which I was previously invested as the core of my identity, and will come to recognise that my values and opinions are not necessarily better than those of others; they are simply different. For the first time, a Self will then emerge which can embrace a truly global world-view.

There are no age norms for this developmental achievement, and very many adults do not attain it because the assistance they need for their growth is not available or because they do not choose to find it. Certainly, work settings which recognise, encourage or support development beyond the Organisational stage are rare indeed – even in those enterprises which are orientated towards learning. Witness the burgeoning business of team development training. It is a common misconception that organisations, as social systems, nurture team behaviour. In fact, more usually, the reverse is true. Most organisations actually nurture their members' *individuality* and, if their leaders are to ameliorate the consequences of this activity (i.e. the members' over-investment in themselves), they will have no alternative but to call continuously upon the services of those whose expertise is helping people to work together more effectively.

If, however, my growth does continue, I will move on to identify with the next stage of development, the World-Centric stage.

World-Centric stage

Organisational stage

Transcending and incorporating the Organisational stage

Identifying with the Organisational stage

SUMMARY *So the organisational adult first* identifies *with her autonomy (becomes fused with it), then* transcends *it by folding it into herself, and then* incorporates *it into her sense of Self (so that she* has *it rather than* is *it) as a capacity for interdependent self-definition arises. If her growth continues, she will move on to identify with a new, higher stage of development: the World-Centric stage.*

*IV. f. The growth and loss of the World-Centric stage.*

ith a world-centric stance, I have transcended completely and irreversibly the socio-centric stages of my development: "…my group is not the only group in the universe, my tribe is not the only tribe, my god is not the only god, my ideology is not the only ideology."[38]

With this level of awareness – that the world is now one territory, one space – I have, at last, achieved the global perspective to which I would only have been able to pay lip service at earlier stages. Systems consultant and global strategist, Louise Diamond, describes this realisation thus:

"Suddenly we understand that truly we are all in this together, and that the boundaries of nation state, individual well-being, and national security are superseded by the transnational flow of information, goods, people, money, and the need to address the well-being of the whole."[39]

In my working environment my new level of functional maturity expresses itself in novel and important ways – in terms of how I manage myself, in terms of how I manage my relationships with others, and in terms of how I exercise my leadership in the wider organisation. So, for example:

At the intra-personal level I can:

+ Pursue self-fulfilment rather than achievement, because I have now separated myself from my activities, whereas I defined myself by them at the former Organisational stage.
+ Give up my certainty for curiosity because 'not knowing' is now a state which does not threaten my sense of who I am.
+ Embrace complexity, paradox, ambiguity, uncertainty and flux because I now know that reality is not defined by *my* wishes, hopes, fears, anxieties, theories and beliefs, or those of my cultural group.

+ Tolerate the shortcomings of myself and others because I now accept human nature for what it is rather than how I would prefer it to be.
+ Acknowledge and cope with the inner conflicts I feel – between conflicting needs, conflicting duties, and the conflict between needs and duties (at work, in life, and between work and life) – because I now understand that they are part of the human condition and I have the courage to deal with them as such.

### At the inter-individual level I can:

+ Learn from anyone who can teach me because I have now renounced my socio-centric stance.
+ Experience deep feelings of connection with, and empathy for, other people because I now realise that we all belong to the same human family.
+ Forge profound, interdependent relationships with them because I now respect, and grant them, their own individuality.
+ Manage my ongoing interactions with them as a complex but fluent series of interpersonal negotiations because my relationships are now important to me for their own sake.
+ Express positive and negative emotions constructively because I now appreciate how my behaviour may create, disrupt or even destroy these relationships.

### At the organisational level I can:

+ Challenge 'business as usual' and find creative solutions to problems because now I am not invested in the preservation of my organisation *as-it-is* as the venue in which I affirm my identity.
+ Evaluate the effect that the organisation is having on the local community, the natural environment, the nation and the world because I now perceive it in the context of the wider system in which it operates.

+ Advance an international rather than a merely multi-national position because I now understand the meaning of a globalised (i.e. an interrelated and interdependent) world.

+ Advocate and defend strong, self-chosen ethical principles in the exercise of my leadership because my moral perspective is now a concern for the welfare of all humankind.

+ Propose a greater purpose for the organisation than to exist simply to maintain itself because I am now able to envision the role it *could* play in the world.†

But the World-Centric stage is the accomplishment of, perhaps, no more than ten per cent of us, as Ken Wilber explains:

"QUESTIONER: We hear a lot about a 'global perspective' or 'global awareness' – think globally, act locally. Most of the 'new paradigm' approaches emphasise that we are living in a global village, a planetary network, and we need a global and systems map to reflect that global territory.

"KEN WILBER: A global map is one thing. A mapmaker capable of living up to it, quite another. A global perspective is not innate; the infant is not born with it; hominids did not possess it. A global perspective is a rare, elite, extraordinary perspective of great depth, and there are relatively few individuals who actually make it to that depth."[40]

Scott Peck describes the implications for humanity as a whole of the widespread failure of individuals to mature beyond the Organisational stage:

"Most of us operate from a narrower frame of reference than

---

† *In Chapter Two we will explore six streams of development – the Intellectual, Social, Moral, Emotional, Psychological and Spiritual streams – which flow through the basic stages of development described in this chapter. It will become apparent through the course of Chapter Two that, in the above list of characteristics, there is a clear indication not just of the stage of development that I have reached, the World-Centric stage, but also of the significant progress I have made along all the developmental streams as well.*

that of which we are capable, failing to transcend the influence of our particular culture, our particular set of parents and our particular childhood experience upon our understanding. It is no wonder, then, that the world of humanity is so full of conflict. We have a situation in which human beings, who must deal with each other, have vastly different views as to the nature of reality, yet each one believes his or her own view to be the correct one since it is based on the microcosm of personal experience. And to make matters worse, most of us are not even fully aware of our world views, much less the uniqueness of the experience from which they are derived…. We are indeed like the three proverbial blind men, each in touch with only his particular piece of the elephant yet each claiming to know the nature of the whole beast. So we squabble over our different microcosmic world views, and all wars are holy wars."[41]

And, yet, there is a further stage to achieve – the Self-Transcendent stage. But, if I am to attain this, I will need to fold into myself my interindividuality, to give up the boundaries of the Self which I have carefully crafted over so many years, and there is, of course, little in the way of external stimulus to prompt me to do so. For this reason, this higher stage of development is a very rare accomplishment indeed.

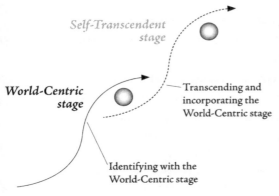

*Self-Transcendent stage*

*World-Centric stage*

Transcending and incorporating the World-Centric stage

Identifying with the World-Centric stage

SUMMARY *So the world-centric adult first identifies with her interindividuality (becomes fused with it). She may then transcend it by folding it into herself, and then incorporate it into her sense of Self (so that she has it rather than is it) if a rare capacity to give up the boundaries of the Self emerges. In the very unlikely event of her growth continuing, she will then move on to identify with a new, higher stage of development: the Self-Transcendent stage.*

### IV. g. The Self-Transcendent stage.

he extraordinary feat of the Self-Transcendent stage involves the emergence of a Self which has achieved a depth of consciousness that is not confined to the ego. Peck, drawing on Hindu and Buddhist teaching, explains:

"...our common perception of the universe as containing multitudes of discrete objects – stars, planets, trees, birds, houses, ourselves – all separated from one another by boundaries is a misperception, an illusion.... True reality can be known only by experiencing the oneness through a giving up of ego boundaries. It is impossible to really see the unity of the universe as long as one continues to see oneself as a discrete object, separate and distinguishable from the rest of the universe in any way, shape or form."[42]

The experience of this higher stage of consciousness is clearly an interior one which cannot be validated by experiments performed in the rational, observable world-space, and which cannot, therefore, be readily described. It is the realm of the sages and the mystics who have variously named it 'Enlightenment', 'Nirvana' or 'The Cloud of Unknowing', and who even attest to there being many sublevels within it, having devised repeatable, contemplative practices which disclose them. I leave the task of enumerating these higher levels to the spiritual guides, for it is they (rather than me) who are best qualified to do so.[43] In passing, however, I note that the character of our questing hero, Parzival, whose story is summarised earlier in this chapter, is derived ultimately from the 'Great Fool' of folk tradition. His conquests, such as they are, clearly do not admit him to the realms of the super-conscious, the Self-Transcendent stage. Writers and readers alike in the medieval period soon, therefore, wanted more from their hero. As the original unfinished story was worked and reworked by many different writers, the Grail, over time, became something beyond the

reach of the ordinary world: it became the 'Holy Grail'. The pursuit of it became a mystical experience, and the achievement of it
a resounding affirmation of the possibilities of the human spirit.
So it was that the chivalric, earthly hero, Parzival, was inevitably
superseded as the Knight of the Grail by a new hero, the spiritually triumphant Galahad.[44]

### *V. Conclusion.*

 e are all embarked on a journey along the human
development road. This road was first charted by
the prophets of the great wisdom traditions.
Modern, orthodox investigators, from their individual viewpoints, have drawn their different but
related maps of it, and, in the foregoing pages, I have offered a

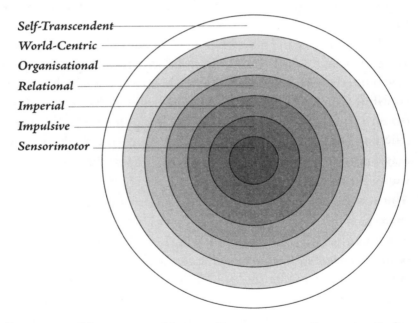

*Self-Transcendent*
*World-Centric*
*Organisational*
*Relational*
*Imperial*
*Impulsive*
*Sensorimotor*

SIMPLIFIED MAP OF THE HUMAN DEVELOPMENT JOURNEY *Earlier,
this journey was represented as the steps of a staircase. It is represented here as a
nest of concentric spheres, which illustrates the two agencies of transcendence and
inclusion by which the stages of the journey unfold.*

simplified account of the human adventure based upon their research.

An abundance of charts and maps exists, therefore, to show us the way, and the theorists agree that the higher stages of development are available to all of us as potentials (barring organic or functional incapacities which can impose restrictions). And yet few of us ever achieve the furthest reaches. The pathway, itself, is difficult to navigate and, moreover, as we shall discover, each stage of the journey offers a particular set of challenges (represented by the never-ending supply of giants, dragons and damsels in distress of the Arthurian world), all of which we must overcome if we are to progress to the next stage of our development as a fully integrated Self. We will explore these manifold challenges in Chapter Two but, before we move on, let us remind ourselves of the main points of this chapter, summarised in a set of simple statements that we might call the 'rules of the road'.

## *The rules of the road.*

1. The human development journey begins in infancy and, if growth continues, may extend into late adulthood and even until death (some, of course, may say that it extends beyond death).
2. The path that we, as travellers, follow is one of many distinct stages, each of which represents a clear, qualitative transformation of thinking and being.
3. The strengths of one stage ultimately become its limitations, a realisation which nudges us to the next stage of our growth.
4. We progress from one stage to the next by the agency of two fundamental capacities: transcendence and inclusion.
5. Research has consistently demonstrated that these stages cannot be bypassed without some compromise.

# FINDING
# MERLIN

*CHAPTER TWO*

# GIANTS
# *AND*
# DRAGONS

*And this meanwhile there came Sir Palomides, the good knight,
following the Questing Beast, that had in shape like a serpent's
head, and a body like a leopard, buttocked like a lion and
footed like a hart; and in his body there was such a
noise as it had been twenty couple of hounds
questing, and such noise that beast made
wheresoever he went. And this beast
evermore Sir Palomides followed,
for it was called his quest.*[1]

LE MORTE DARTHUR
Thomas Malory

## · CHAPTER TWO ·
# Giants and Dragons

### I. The questing beast.

n Chapter One, the human adventure was represented as a journey along a road of many stages of self-identity and self-growth. It is a road which has been well mapped yet few of us attain its furthest reaches. The pathway, itself, is difficult to navigate and, as we shall discover in this chapter, each stage of the journey offers its own set of challenges (intellectual, social, moral, emotional, psychological and even spiritual challenges), all of which we must overcome if we are to progress to the next stage of our development as a fully integrated Self.

These 'issues to be confronted'[2] flow as *streams* through the basic *stages* of development. Cross-cultural empirical studies demonstrate that the streams unfold in the same way as the stages unfold – as clear, qualitative *transformations of thinking and being*, and by the same processes of *transcendence* and *inclusion*. The two now familiar catalysts of maturational brain changes and the experience of phenomena which do not conform to our existing ideologies nudge us towards more sophisticated levels of functional maturity and, as with the stages of development, none of these levels can be bypassed without compromise.† The summation of our achievements in these streams indicates the overall stage of development that we have reached.

Importantly, the streams of development emerge with their own dynamic – in both a dependent and an independent relation-

---

† *In the knight errant quest, the hero's Search for Self is not an easy one. As he makes his way along the forest paths he is continually waylaid by strange and fearsome creatures, wrathful villains, and damsels in need of deliverance. None of these obstacles can be avoided if he is to travel onwards.*

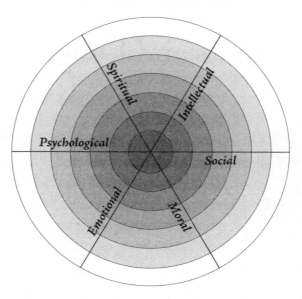

AN INTEGRAL MODEL OF DEVELOPMENT *The intellectual, social, moral, emotional, psychological and even spiritual challenges that confront us on our journey flow through the basic developmental stages (described in Chapter One) as* streams of development. *They also unfold as the stages unfold — by the processes of transcendence and inclusion. We navigate this complex landscape along a spiralling pathway which integrates our achievements in all the developmental streams. The summation of our achievements in these streams indicates the overall stage of development that we have reached.*

ship with each other. If, in our determination to press onwards (driven by our own volition or the demands of our world to move forward quickly), we choose not to address the full range of challenges presented to us at our current stage, we will arrive at the next stage of our journey with some of our potential unrealised, with an imbalance in our sphere of total capability. The further we travel along the pathway of growth, of course, the greater the risk of such developmental gaps appearing, and such gaps will necessarily place limitations on us as we try to manage the ever-more complex circumstances and events of our organisational lives.

To function as a fully integrated Self, therefore, we must seek

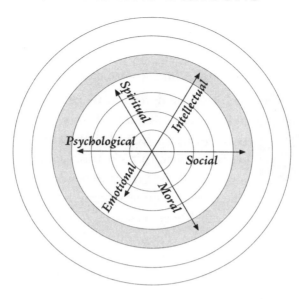

THE DEVELOPMENT OF AN INDIVIDUAL *who has reached the Organisational stage of growth (indicated by the shaded ring) and who has overcome many of the challenges in the Intellectual, Social and Moral streams which are associated with it, but who has work to do in the Emotional, Psychological and Spiritual domains if he or she is to function at this stage as a fully integrated Self.*

out those stream-specific learning experiences which will enable us to attend to our particular developmental gaps. As we know from Chapter One, our neurology is, of course, ready-primed for this work, and Peter Reason, an investigator in the practice of action research, offers some words of encouragement:

"...if you are clear with your intent and work as well as you are able towards it, the universe does seem to bring opportunities that can be seized. The attitude needed is one of control and surrender, bringing discipline to the work while always watching for the unplanned opportunities that arise and being willing to go with them, riding the wave."[3]

In the following pages, six streams of development are described – the streams which are the most important to us in our organisational lives.[4]

## II. *The Streams of development.*

### II. a. *The Intellectual Stream of development.*

he Intellectual stream describes the process of making sense of data – how we absorb it, organise it, interpret it, and then take action upon it. We begin with this stream because it is upon this one that all the others depend: we construct our knowledge of all the domains of development by reflecting upon, and understanding, our life experiences. Cognitive development is, therefore, central to the whole course of our growth.

The pioneering epistemologist, Jean Piaget, was instrumental in mapping the Intellectual stream as it unfolds in phases of increasing levels of sophistication from birth to adulthood. For over half a century, from 1920, he made detailed observations of children's activities, talking to them, listening to them talking to each other, and devising and presenting many 'tests' of children's thinking.

Piaget identified four distinct phases of intellectual development: the sensorimotor level; the level of preoperational thought; the level of concrete operations; and the level of formal operations.

I am born into the sensorimotor level, into an objectless world in which everything sensed is taken to be an extension of me and where 'out of sight' (or touch or taste or hearing or smell) can mean 'out of existence' (see also the description of the Sensorimotor stage in Chapter One which corresponds to this level of the Intellectual stream). The main achievements of my intelligence during my first eighteen months are to differentiate myself from the external world (the discovery *that* I am), and to construct 'the permanence of the object' (to understand that objects can exist even when they are not visible), whereupon I attain, typically by the age of two, the level of preoperational thought.

During this pre-school period, I am indeed able to recognise objects as separate from myself, but they are subject to my own perception of them: if my perception of an object changes, the object itself has changed, in my experience (see the Impulsive stage). This phase of preoperational thought was studied extensively by Piaget through his famous 'conservation tasks', where 'conservation' means the understanding (which I have yet to acquire) that objects remain the same in relation to some fundamental characteristic such as number, mass, weight or volume, even though changes in shape or arrangement may occur. So, for example, if I participate in his well-known experiment relating to the conservation of liquids in which the contents of a glass A are poured into a narrower glass B, as a four-to-six-year-old (i.e. a preoperational child) I will think that the liquid increases in quantity as it is poured from glass A to glass B because the level of the liquid is higher in B than it was in A.[5]

But gradually, between the ages of five and seven, I become capable of distinguishing between how something *appears* and how something *is*. In the words of Robert Kegan, "The world which before was so labile starts to hold still; it becomes concrete",[6] and so I attain the level of concrete operations. I am now very engaged with this world, seeking to understand it and master it. This is the era of questions about facts and figures, about how things work, about causes and effects; and Piaget, as a result of his tests, asserts that conservation takes place in a definite order with conservation of number occurring at approximately six or seven years, of mass at seven years, of weight at nine years, and of volume at about eleven or twelve years. (So, in the experiment described above, as a twelve-year-old I would understand that the amount of liquid does not change when it is poured from glass A to glass B.)

My thinking processes at this level are very logical, and the inferences I draw tend to be mechanistic and absolute – it is always wrong to lie, for example. But in the years prior to puberty,

I gradually acquire another new and profound intellectual capacity. Formerly, my awareness was only able to operate on the concrete world. Now it is able to operate on thought itself – I can reflect upon my thinking. The psychologist, Jerome Kagan, employs a syllogism to illustrate this important developmental achievement: "The twelve-year-old will accept and think about the following problem: 'All three-legged snakes are purple, I am hiding a three-legged snake, guess its colour?'" On the other hand, "[t]he seven-year-old is confused by the fact that the initial premises violate his notion of what is real and he will not cooperate.... To appreciate that problems can be self-contained entities solved by special rules is a magnificent accomplishment that is not usually attained until early adolescence."[7]

So I can now generate hypothetical explanations for situations, and solutions to problems. I can also imagine "What if...?", as Ken Wilber explains:

"All sorts of idealistic possibilities open up, and the person's awareness can dream of things that are not yet, and picture future worlds of ideal possibilities, and work to change the world according to those dreams. You can imagine what yet might be!"[8]

True introspection becomes available to me, too. This is the level of formal operations, of abstract thinking (and an intellectual achievement which is, incidentally, an essential one for organisational leaders who need to envisage scenarios and possibilities which do not exist yet in the concrete world, and to formulate ideas for working with, and taking advantage of, them). The emergence of this final phase of intellectual development commences when I am about eleven years old and is completed by my late teens, although we should note that several studies have revealed that only sixty per cent of adults in Western countries ever use formal operational thinking and that those who do do not employ it consistently.

Some subsequent researchers have suggested that Piaget may have underestimated the cognitive abilities of babies and young

children. He has also been criticised for paying insufficient attention to the role that the environment, emotions and social factors play in child development – aspects we will consider later in
this chapter. Cross-cultural studies of children in many different
countries have supported his findings, however, and his theory
remains influential in cognitive developmental research.[9] In the
meantime, there is much interest in the academic arena in the
possibility of higher levels of intellectual development being available to us beyond formal operations. The identity theorist, Jane
Loevinger, for example, observes an increasing capacity for conceptual sophistication throughout adulthood, enabling us, ultimately, to be able to embrace complexity, paradox and ambiguity[10]
(and I would add 'uncertainty' and 'flux' to this list). The developmental psychologist, Gisela Labouvie-Vief, has proposed a level of
post-formal thought which is less of an objective, impersonal and
rational activity, and more of a subjective, interpersonal and non-
rational one.[11] And the physicist and philosopher, David Bohm,
has described a very distinctive and exceptional facility to participate in *group* thinking. This is a cognitive process which requires
those involved to give up (i.e. to cease defending) their own
assumptions and opinions, to allow shared meaning to emerge[12]
– a process which will enable them, thereby, to attend to those
'wicked problems'† and 'social messes' which present so frequently

---

† A 'wicked problem' (formally described in 1973 by the design theorists, Horst
Rittel and Melvin M. Webber, and generalised in 2006 by the researcher in collaborative technology, Jeff Conklin) is a complex problem involving many stakeholders of differing perspectives who need to develop a shared understanding of each
others' positions in order to exercise collective intelligence to solve it. A 'tame problem' is one which can be addressed by the traditional, analytical, linear processes
of formal operational thinking such as solving a mathematical problem, analysing
the structure of a chemical compound or achieving 'checkmate' in five moves in
a game of chess. A 'social mess' (described by the political scientist, Robert Horn,
extending the work of organisational theorist, Russell L. Ackoff) is a system of
problems defined by characteristics such as ideological, cultural, political and economic constraints, numerous possible intervention points, considerable uncertainty and ambiguity, and great resistance to change.

TYPICAL ACHIEVEMENTS OF THE
# INTELLECTUAL STREAM

| Age / Stage | Principal intellectual tasks |
|---|---|
| Infancy<br>*Sensorimotor stage* | ❖ The awareness of 'Self'<br>❖ The construction of object permanence |
| Early childhood<br>*Impulsive stage* | ❖ Magical thought processes |
| Middle to<br>late childhood<br>*Imperial stage* | ❖ Logical thought processes |
| Adolescence<br>*Relational stage* | ❖ Abstract thought processes, i.e. the capacity to reflect upon Self, one's experiences and one's thinking (one's own thoughts and ideas) |
| Young adulthood<br>and beyond<br>*Organisational stage* | ❖ An increasing capacity for conceptual thinking |
| Mid-life<br>and beyond<br>*World-Centric<br>stage* | ❖ Conceptual sophistication (enabling oneself, for example, to engage in subjective, interpersonal and non-rational thought processes, and to embrace complexity, paradox, ambiguity, uncertainty and flux)<br>*Then, if growth continues at this stage:*<br>❖ The capacity to participate in group thinking |

to all of us in our living and working as members of an inter-related and interdependent global community. To date, empirical evidence is lacking to substantiate these various hypotheses, but they deserve our recognition as exciting propositions that our own experience may validate. The theory, in other words, may be lagging behind our real-world knowledge and practice.

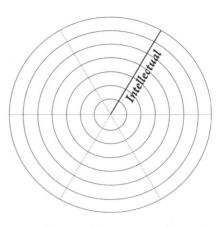

Summary *The Intellectual stream describes the process of making sense of data – how we absorb, organise, interpret, and take action upon it – and it is central to the whole course of our growth. Four levels of intellectual development, which unfold from infancy through to our late teens, have been well mapped by Jean Piaget and other neo-Piagetian and post-Piagetian researchers. Whether or not levels beyond formal operations are available to us we do not yet know; there is certainly much interest in the academic arena in this possibility. We can be confident, however, that, if further levels are confirmed, environmental phenomena will prove to be the catalyst for them. In the meantime, it is important to note that some individuals never attain full formal operations. Our challenge in adulthood, therefore, is to ensure that we do, for, without the capacity to reflect upon ourselves, our experiences and our thinking (i.e. our own thoughts and ideas), our progress through all the domains of development will be limited indeed.*

## II. b. The Social stream of development.

he Social stream describes the process of forging social connection, of discovering how to relate to, adapt to, and function with, other people.[13] It follows the Intellectual stream because our relationships are also foundational to our overall development, shaping both the structure of the brain and the emergence of the mind, as the psychologist, Daniel Siegel, explains.[14] Interactions with the environment, *especially within interpersonal relationships*, govern the genetically programmed maturation of the central nervous system (as described in Chapter One of this book). And the mental models of Self, and of the Self with others, which we create through our social involvements, form an 'essential scaffold' for the development of our psyche. (Those rare and widely reported instances of children who are discovered in states of extreme deprivation, having had little or no contact with other human beings, illustrate the foundational nature of the Social stream. Invariably, these children lack the normal skills of social intercourse, and their growth is severely and permanently retarded.)

Social development is an exciting and dynamic process but a complex one, too – in part because it occurs within the framework of our personal relationships, involving input from both parties, and in part because it is mediated by our individual cultural context with its particular systems of beliefs and attitudes, and its own (often gender-specific) rules of behaviour. No unifying theory or all-embracing stage-sequence classification for the field has yet been proposed. The following summary is drawn from a masterful review of current knowledge by Kevin Durkin[15], organised into a series of principal, age-related social tasks which I offer to readers as a simple, overarching structure to describe our progress through the Social stream.

The process of creating connection with others begins at birth.[16] I enter the world well equipped to react to my social environment, which, in turn, accommodates to me, transforming my capacities into meaningful participation. As a baby, I have disproportionately large eyes and a head-to-body ratio generally greater than that of a mature human – features which are arousing to adults. Through my signalling reflexes (crying and, later, smiling), I can transmit my physical needs to my carers who are, typically, able and motivated to deal with them. Very quickly, I show a preference for the human voice over other noises and, long before I can speak, I appear to enjoy vocal interchanges with those around me, preparing me for the development of that fundamental mode of human interaction: conversation.†

By three months, I can distinguish one person from another: I have an awareness of 'the other', which is clearly an essential skill

† *Depriving people of the opportunity for conversation is a naturally discovered social sanction which is applied both informally (through 'silent treatment') and formally (through solitary confinement) to dramatic effect upon the recipient.*

for building relationship. And by the age of eleven months, I am beginning to demonstrate secure attachments† to specific individuals (usually my primary caregivers) and anxiety in the presence of strangers. Studies from around the world have demonstrated the universal relevance of this attachment construct. The formation and the nature of these first relationships are regarded as crucial because they represent the context within which I will develop my initial social skills, in readiness for my interaction with a wider social environment.[17] As Siegel explains:

"At the level of the mind, attachment establishes an interpersonal relationship that helps the immature brain use the mature functions of the parent's brain to organise its own processes."[18]

In particular, my emerging awareness of 'the other' in a securely attached caregiving relationship fosters the development of empathy, the capacity to know what that other person is experiencing and to respond appropriately. (And this capacity will, as we shall discover in the following sections, prove to be essential if I am to progress along not just this, the Social stream, but along the Moral, Emotional, Psychological and Spiritual streams as well.)

So my caregivers are, self-evidently, the principal contributors to my early socialisation during my pre-school years, but my siblings afford me many opportunities to practise my social skills, too:

"Young siblings fight with one another. They provoke and irritate one another with devastating lack of inhibition. They amuse and excite one another and engage in uproarious games together. They comfort and care for one another. No psychologist is needed to point out the passion, fury and jealousy, the range of emotion

---

† *From the important work of John Bowlby, and other theorists in the field of developmental psychology (notably Mary Ainsworth), a typology of four attachment relationships has been developed. This typology comprises three types of insecure attachment (Avoidant, Resistant, and Disorganised and Disorientated) and one type of secure attachment (Secure, which, research suggests, seventy per cent of infants achieve). The antecedent for these different attachment relationships is likely to be the quality of caregiving[19] – see Chapter Five.*

from gentle sympathy to wild aggression, that is expressed so uninhibitedly by siblings in their first three years."[20]

In most societies, I will also interact with children outside my immediate nuclear family from very early in life for I can enjoy peer relationships from just three months. These interactions increase in frequency and quality as I approach school age, becoming complex patterns of interchange which are communicated primarily through the important vehicle of non-verbal behaviour as language is not yet well developed.[21]

During my primary school years, I acquire a more and more sophisticated understanding of other people, relationships and interpersonal expectations. I also have more advanced linguistic abilities which broaden my scope for conversation. My pro-social behaviour – giving, sharing, co-operating, protecting and so on[22] – strengthens during this period (with pro-social tendency being a reasonably good predictor of social adjustment). At this point, real friendships begin to emerge, which also foster the growth of social competence – and there are potential liabilities for me if I am not able to make and sustain them. 'Social competence' is difficult to define (not least because it is clearly mediated by culture) but one influential model, proposed by the psychologist, Kenneth A. Dodge, et al, suggests that it involves the successful application of five sequential steps[23]:

1. Encoding the presented social cues (e.g. a peer's facial expression).
2. Representing the cues mentally and interpreting them in an accurate and meaningful way.
3. Generating one or more potential behavioural responses to the interpreted clues (even a young child has a repertoire of many possible responses).
4. Evaluating the probable efficacy and consequences of the responses which have been generated, and selecting an optimal choice.
5. Enacting the chosen response in behaviour.

The application of these five sequential steps is assumed to occur very rapidly in real time and often at a non-conscious level. Importantly, deficiencies at any one step can result in less than optimal social behaviour.

The place of peers expands further during my adolescence as I move into more diverse settings away from my parentally controlled environment – indeed my interpersonal relationships with peers are central to my development during this period of my life as I practise the age-related and gender-related norms of adolescent behaviour as they are defined for me by my cultural context.[24]

And the importance of attachments generally – and of strong friendships and romantic relationships in particular – is maintained during my adulthood, too. One of the benefits of attachments at any age is that they afford a secure base from which to tackle life's stresses but, as noted above, relationships are also, of themselves, fundamentally developmental, involving ongoing adjustments which promote the attainment of full social competence. Even the initiation of a long-term partnership is the outcome not just of sexual attraction but of a complex series of social negotiations between me and him or her. And, even when I am

> "Who one is, how one changes, where one is going are all dependent upon relations with others & upon how one responds to the expectations of the social world."[25]
> DURKIN

in these partnerships, the negotiations continue – for no relationship, however strong, is ever completely 'static'. Other events in my life cycle (such as entering or leaving the workforce, marriage or divorce, the transition to parenthood, the experience of the 'empty nest' or, conversely, the 'crowded nest', broadening involvement in the community, or the death of my partner or someone I love) may also have substantial consequences for my relations with others, requiring new accommodations. And, again, all these adjustments occur in the context of a broader society which is transmitting culturally specific, socially shared beliefs about how I should behave in the different phases of my adult life.[26]

TYPICAL ACHIEVEMENTS OF THE
# SOCIAL STREAM

| Age / Stage | Principal social tasks |
|---|---|
| Infancy<br>*Sensorimotor stage* | ❖ An awareness of 'the other'<br>❖ Secure attachments to specific individuals |
| Early childhood<br>*Impulsive stage* | ❖ Early socialisation |
| Middle to<br>late childhood<br>*Imperial stage* | ❖ Pro-social behaviour |
| Adolescence<br>*Relational stage* | ❖ Interpersonal relationships |
| Young adulthood<br>and beyond<br>*Organisational stage* | ❖ Social competence (i.e. the ability to relate to, adapt to, and function with, other people) |
| Mid-life and beyond<br>*World-Centric stage* | ❖ Continuous honing of one's social skills |

In old age, this challenge to remain an actively involved social being acquires a new imperative for me, notwithstanding the difficulties presented by my physical decline and negative stereotypes. Social involvement generally predicts well-being and positive adaptation to events – even to some of the most painful events – of later life. Women tend to rise to this challenge more easily than men. Ties between women are described by researchers as stronger, more frequent and more reciprocal; men, on the other hand, report that they find it difficult to achieve psychological intimacy outside the home (which is one reason why widowers may be more likely to remarry than widows).[27]

SUMMARY The *Social* stream describes the process of forging social connection, of discovering how to relate to, adapt to, and function with, other people. As a group-living, socially dependent species, our lives are grounded in our relationships. They are also the venue for much of our growth through all the streams of development because they shape both the structure of the brain and the emergence of the mind. No grand, unifying theory has yet been proposed to describe how we become socially competent but, as Kevin Durkin explains, this process begins at birth, is mediated by our cultural context, and proceeds through the lifespan since progress through life inevitably involves entering new relationships, accepting new roles, adjusting to new circumstances in our community, and so on. The challenge the Social stream presents to us in adulthood, therefore, is to treat these experiences not simply as external events which happen to us, but as opportunities for ongoing learning in our continually changing social environment – involvements which are, in Durkin's words, "at the core of being human".[28]

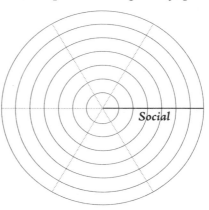

## II. c. The Moral stream of development.

he Moral stream describes the process of acquiring moral reasoning – our increasingly sophisticated understanding of what is 'right' and what is 'wrong'.[29] It follows the Social stream, not because moral development is a product of socialisation (i.e. socialising agents such as parents or educators teaching new forms of thinking) but because, as we enter into discussions and debates with others (particularly in situations where we take the role of 'the other' and appreciate events from the other's point of view), our ethical judgements are questioned and challenged, and we are motivated to create new, more comprehensive positions.[30]

Philosophers from the East and the West, from Confucius (551–479 BCE) and Aristotle (384–322 BCE) onwards, have been interested in this field of study. "Many important and difficult questions arise in the course of a human life," writes A.C. Grayling, "but few can compare with the most significant question any individual can ask, namely, 'How shall I live, in order to live a good life?'"[31] Psychologists have also been investigating it for many years and, in 1958, Lawrence Kohlberg proposed an integrated classification of moral development (modifying and elaborating upon some early work by Jean Piaget). His technique involved presenting subjects with a moral dilemma in story form, and then asking them to decide what action a person should take in such a dilemma and *why* (so he was curious about their rationale). On the basis of his research, he identified six moral perspectives grouped into three major levels, with each level representing a fundamental shift in the moral understanding of the individual.[32]

At the first, pre-conventional level, a morality of constraint applies in which we, as young children typically aged between four and ten years, view morality as something which is external to ourselves, imposed by those with sufficient power over us to exercise punishment or reward, or to secure the exchange of favours. At the second, conventional level, a morality of convention applies, in which we, as adolescents, view the expectations and rules (of our family, group or nation) as contributing to the maintenance of social order. The third, post-conventional level is characterised by a major thrust towards autonomous moral principles, a process which begins with the perception of relativism, the awareness that any given society's definition of right and wrong, however legitimate, is only one among many. Kohlberg's research suggests that most adults do not achieve this third level of moral development.

So, as I am emerging from the Impulsive stage, typically at the age of four, I discover that there are rules (of which I was previously unaware) which must be observed. Accordingly, I judge whether an action is right or wrong in terms of whether it is consistent with these rules, and in terms of whether I will be punished for it by those in authority over me, whose standpoint I cannot separate from my own. This is the first moral position of Kohlberg's classification system, the punishment and obedience orientation.

But gradually, between the ages of five and seven, as a self-concept emerges and I become invested in satisfying my personal needs (see the Imperial stage), I begin to judge whether an action is right or wrong according to whether or not it meets these needs. My concern does extend to 'my group' so I give *some* consideration to the interests of those who belong to it *if* the result is favourable to me – 'right' can be what is fair, what is an equal exchange, a deal, or an agreement. I will continue to observe the rules imposed by figures of authority but only where they serve my own ends. This is the second moral position, the self-interest orientation.

As an adolescent, I learn to co-ordinate my needs (in which I was previously so invested) with the interests of others (see the Relational stage) and I become orientated towards mutuality. Shared feelings, agreements and expectations take primacy. I need to be a 'good' person in my own eyes and in the eyes of all: the Golden Rule is my guiding principle.† I now judge whether an action is right or wrong according to whether or not it is motivated by good intentions. This is the third moral position, the good interpersonal relationships orientation.

As a young adult, I acquire a 'system perspective' and become concerned with how society functions as a whole. Right behaviour consists of doing one's duty, showing respect for authority, and maintaining the given social order for its own sake. Laws are to be upheld except in extreme cases where they conflict with other fixed social duties. This is the fourth moral position, the law and order orientation.

If my moral development continues to unfold in adulthood, I

† *The Golden Rule (or the Ethic of Reciprocity) is a principle of ethical conduct which has a long history in philosophy and the world's religions, and refers to doing to others as you would have them do to you.*

will, in time, become aware that people hold a variety of values and opinions, and that most rules are relative to the group concerned. I now believe that these rules must be upheld in the interest of impartiality, and because they are the social contract. But I also believe that some non-relative rights (e.g. the right to life, or the right to liberty) must be upheld in *any* society regardless of the majority opinion: the welfare of all is my concern. As the developmental psychologist, Carol Gilligan, asserts:

"...it is not tenable... to adopt a position of ethical neutrality or cultural relativism – to say that one cannot say anything about values or that all values are culturally relative. Such a hands-off stance in the face of atrocity amounts to a kind of complicity."[33]

So, I can, and do, make distinctions about which philosophies and ideologies are more inclusive and more conducive to the development of humankind. Right action, therefore, tends to be defined in terms of what makes for a 'good' society – standards which have been critically examined and generally agreed upon for the betterment of society. (At my previous perspective, the law was 'fixed'; at this perspective, the law may be changed if it conflicts with rational considerations of social utility.) This is the fifth moral position, the social contract orientation.

As a mature adult, it may transpire that I acquire a belief in the validity of a set of universal ethical principles (of justice, of the reciprocity and equality of human rights, and of respect for the dignity of human beings as individual persons) which I formulate for myself. When laws conflict with these self-chosen (i.e. unconventional) principles, I act in accordance with them. (At my previous perspective, I was hesitant to endorse civil disobedience because the social contract should only be changed through democratic means; at this perspective, my commitment to these universal principles carries with it an obligation to disobey unjust rules.) This is the sixth moral position, the universal principles orientation, and is so rare an achievement that Kohlberg eventually dropped it from his classification system.

A number of criticisms of Kohlberg's work have been made.[34] Gilligan, a former co-worker of Kohlberg, suggests that his conception of morality, derived from male-only interviews, is too narrow, reflecting a clear male sex bias. She asserts that for males, who are socialised to be independent and achievement-orientated, advanced moral thought revolves around rules, rights and abstract principles, which *are* reflected in Kohlberg's stages. For women, however, who are socialised to nurture and maintain a sense of responsibility towards others, morality centres not on rights and rules but on interpersonal relationships and the ethics of compassion and care, which are *not* reflected in Kohlberg's stages.[35] Whilst subsequent research has not revealed a significant difference in male and female moral reasoning, Gilligan's work has certainly contributed to the debate about what morality is and how it should be measured. For the psychologist, Elliot Turiel, Kohlberg's conception of morality is too broad inasmuch as he fails to distinguish between morality and social convention, a distinction that, he demonstrates, even very young children can make. His research, therefore, challenges Kohlberg's claim that young children are, essentially, amoral (i.e. without access to moral reasoning).[36] More recently, critics have focused on the complex interrelationship between morality and ideology, asserting that Kohlberg's stages are an endorsement of the liberal-humanist Western philosophical tradition. Notwithstanding these criticisms, cross-cultural and longitudinal studies involving thousands of people of all ages, intelligence levels and socio-economic backgrounds, have demonstrated much support for the universality of Kohlberg's stages, and his theory continues to dominate the discussion about how our increasingly sophisticated understanding of what is 'right' and what is 'wrong' unfolds through the lifespan.

SUMMARY *The Moral stream describes the process of acquiring moral reasoning which occurs, necessarily, in relationship with others: as we interact with others, and learn to appreciate the thinking of others, our moral assumptions are challenged and we achieve new, more comprehensive positions. Lawrence*

TYPICAL ACHIEVEMENTS OF THE
# MORAL STREAM

| Age / Stage | Principal moral tasks |
|---|---|
| Infancy<br>*Sensorimotor stage* | – |
| Early childhood<br>*Impulsive stage* | ❖ The definition of an action as 'right' or 'wrong' according to whether or not it is consistent with the rules, and whether or not punishment will follow |
| Middle to late childhood<br>*Imperial stage* | ❖ The definition of an action as 'right' or 'wrong' according to whether or not it serves one's own needs |
| Adolescence<br>*Relational stage* | ❖ The definition of an action as 'right' or 'wrong' according to whether or not it pleases or helps others, and is approved by them |
| Young adulthood and beyond<br>*Organisational stage* | ❖ The definition of an action as 'right' or 'wrong' according to whether or not it maintains the given social order |
| Mid-life and beyond<br>*World-Centric stage* | ❖ The definition of an action as 'right' or 'wrong' according to whether or not it makes for a good society (this requires a recognition that one's own reference group's definition of 'right' and 'wrong' is only one among many, plus a preparedness to make distinctions about which ethical principles are the most conducive to the development of humankind)<br>*Then, if growth continues at this stage:*<br>❖ Self-chosen ethical principles and a preparedness to take action to defend them |

*Kohlberg mapped six developmental perspectives which reflect an expansion in moral understanding from an individual, to a societal, to a universal point of view. These perspectives are available to all of us as potentials, although few of us, it seems, reach the most advanced, post-conventional level of discernment and, even when we do, we may not act in accordance with our ethical judgements, for none of us, however highly we regard ourselves, is ever wholly morally coherent. Our*

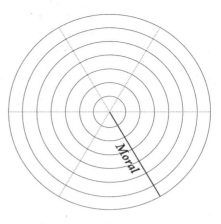

*opportunity, therefore, in adulthood is to continue to question our assumptions about what is 'right' and what is 'wrong' until we reach that principled position where we respect the dignity of every human being, and know that human rights pertain to all — and where, of course, we can defend that position in action, if necessary, as well as in words.*

## II. d. The Emotional Stream of development.

he Emotional stream describes the process of managing our responses to emotionally arousing stimuli. To know our feelings is a uniquely human possibility.[37] But knowing our feelings, whilst necessary, is not sufficient for our emotional development. We must also learn to manage our behaviour in relation to them, to recognise them as a cue to create choices for how we should respond to the stimuli we are experiencing. The Emotional stream follows the Intellectual, Social and Moral streams because our ability to regulate our emotional reactions is linked directly to our capacity to be aware, intentionally, not just of ourselves, but of ourselves in connection with others, and with the rest of the world.

We know our emotions – fear, anger, disgust, joy and so on[38] – by their intrusions (welcome or otherwise) into our conscious minds but, as the psychologist and pre-eminent researcher, Joseph LeDoux, describes, emotions did not evolve as conscious feelings.

They emerged, instead, as brain states and bodily responses. Each emotion primes us to act in service of the main project of evolution: to survive in hostile environments in order to procreate. At a minimum, we need to obtain food and shelter, defend ourselves from danger, secure a mate and protect our offspring; and it is our emotions, operating outside consciousness, which trigger our physical responses when we are faced with circumstances that threaten those primary functions. But in the modern world, a world which for many of us is less hostile than that of our ancestors, our emotions do not always serve us well, as LeDoux explains:

"When fear becomes anxiety, desire gives way to greed, or annoyance turns to anger, anger to hatred, friendship to envy, love to obsession, or pleasure to addiction, our emotions start working against us."[39]

And all of us experience these highly charged, destructive emotional states from time to time. Why is this so?

Different emotions are mediated by separate neural systems but LeDoux has proposed that all emotional responses are effects which are likely to be caused by the activity of a common underlying system: the amygdala, a small almond-shaped region in the forebrain. Through his research into the fear system of the brain, he has identified that it is in the amygdala where trigger-stimuli (situations of significance, signalled by information built into the brain by evolution or by memories of past events) do their triggering.[40]

LeDoux describes two pathways – the 'low road' and the 'high road' – along which information about external stimuli reaches the amygdala.

Incoming sensory signals are translated into the language of the brain in the thalamus. The largest allocation of this message then passes to the cortex along the 'high road', where the higher processing systems of the brain are positioned, and where detailed and accurate representations of the incoming information are

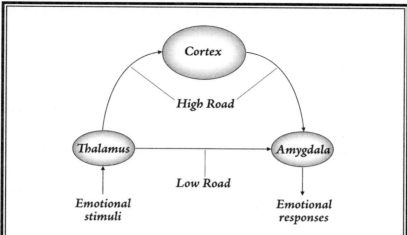

**THE LOW ROAD AND THE HIGH ROAD TO THE AMYGDALA**[41]
*As an example from everyday experience, perhaps you recall being awakened suddenly at night by a noise? You are already tense at the point of awakening, and are poised to jump out of bed and run to grab a fire poker or a cricket bat. As you lie there in a state of full alert you hear the noise for a second time and realise that it is the window blinds rattling in a gust of wind. You begin to relax and eventually fall asleep again. In just a few moments you have experienced the emergency response of the low road, succeeded by the reasoned response of the high road.*

generated. From here, a reasoned interpretation of the stimulus is transmitted to the amygdala, where our physical responses are activated. But another allocation of the original message passes along the 'low road' – a shorter, direct transmission route from the thalamus to the amygdala. As this emergency pathway bypasses the cortex, it can only supply the amygdala with a crude representation of the stimulus. The advantage it provides is that it enables us to respond to a potentially threatening event before we even recognise the stimulus for what it is.† This neural mech-

---

† *"From the point of view of survival, it is better to respond to potentially dangerous events as if they were in fact the real thing than to fail to respond. The cost of treating a stick as a snake is less, in the long run, than the cost of treating a snake as a stick."*[42] *– LeDoux*

anism, which is highly conserved through many levels of evolutionary history, can be very useful to us in dangerous situations, but its utility requires that the cortical pathway be able to override the direct pathway in situations which are not. And, for all of us, there are times – many times – when we are unable to control our emotional reactions, with irrational, even pathological, consequences. The psychologist, Daniel Goleman, observes:

"…passions overwhelm reason time and again. This given of human nature arises from the basic architecture of mental life. In terms of biological design for the basic neural circuitry of emotion, what we are born with is what worked best for the last 50,000 human generations, not the last 500 generations – and certainly not the last five…. In short, we too often confront postmodern dilemmas with an emotional repertoire tailored to the urgencies of the Pleistocene."[43]

The ongoing challenge of the Emotional stream is, therefore, in Goleman's words, to manage our emotional life with intelligence – which is no mean feat given that most of the emotional activity of the brain occurs in the emotional unconscious.† As Aristotle, referring specifically to the emotion of anger, remarks in an oft-quoted phrase, "Anyone can become angry – that is easy. But to be angry with the right person, to the right degree, at the right time, for the right purpose, and in the right way – this is not easy."[44] A comprehensive theory has yet to be proposed to describe how emotional development unfolds through the lifespan but, by drawing on the work of the psychologist, L. Alan Sroufe, who focuses on the organisation of emotional life in the early years,[45] plus that of the aforementioned Joseph LeDoux and Daniel Goleman, I summarise the emergence of a competent

---

† *"A father who yells at his children may rationalize his outburst by saying that the children were misbehaving. But the outburst may also be due in part to the fact that he had a bad day at the office, or even to the way his parents treated him as a child, and at the time he may not be consciously aware of these influences at all."*[46] *– LeDoux*

emotional being in a simple overarching structure of age-related principal tasks, as follows.

Emotions proper do not exist in the newborn period. In these early weeks of my life, prior to the maturation of my limbic structures and especially my corticolimbic interconnections, it is likely that I only experience undifferentiated positive and negative arousal in response to stimulation. But, by three months, precursor emotional responses such as pleasure, wariness and frustration are emerging as diffuse reactions (smiling, cooing, twisting, turning, kicking) to broad classes of stimulation.[47]

By ten months, I have, of course, discovered 'Self' as a separate entity from my surroundings. With the capacity to distinguish my inner experience from external events, I become aware of my subjective feelings and I am also able to evaluate the situations which gave rise to these feelings. I can express the basic emotions of fear, anger, disgust and joy, with their distinctive biological signatures, as more precise, immediate and meaningful reactions, which are qualitatively different from earlier, precursor expressions.

At this point, it may be helpful to clarify the terminology of 'emotions' and 'feelings'. Emotions, as LeDoux has demonstrated, happen to us – we do not will them to occur; feelings result when we become consciously aware that an emotion system of the brain is active. "The brain states and bodily responses are the fundamental facts of an emotion, and the conscious feelings are the frills that have added icing to the emotional cake."[48]

> EMOTION:
> *a brain state and a bodily response, both of which operate outside consciousness and are triggered by an emotionally arousing stimulus.*
>
> ———
>
> FEELING:
> *an interpretation of the stimulus in the cortex – as being either positive, neutral or negative.*

During my second year, as we know, I discover that 'Self' and 'others' are independent agents, a discovery which promotes my ability to express primitive forms of more complex emotions such as pride, guilt, affection and shame. Pride and guilt, for example, require a comparison with an internalised standard of behaviour; affection can only be experienced by a well-differentiated 'Self' with regard to a clearly represented 'other'; and shame requires an audience.[49] I also become capable of moods (i.e. my responses to external circumstances fluctuate less rapidly) and so I can be more purposeful in communicating my feelings.

Throughout these years of infancy, my caregivers are central to my emotional development. Initially, they have total responsibility for keeping arousal within tolerable limits for me: when the degree of tension surpasses my capacities, they modify the situation. In time, however, I play an increasing role in a dyadic regulation process. I use my caregiver relationships to learn to tolerate and modulate tension, by eliciting assistance when I have exceeded my current limits for managing myself and need support to restore equilibrium.[50]

During my toddler period, greater self-awareness (awareness of my internal states and bodily sensations), the advent of language (which enables me to identify and name my emotions), and an increasing ability to soothe myself when I am upset, facilitate the beginnings of self-control. Within certain boundaries, I am much more capable of regulating my responses than I was as an infant – I can fight down tears or exhibit angry feelings in subtle and indirect ways. But stronger impulses easily overwhelm me, and so my caregivers continue to be important: they talk to me about my feelings and how to understand them, and they problem-solve with me when I am in emotional predicaments. This is a time of *guided* self-regulation.[51]

During my pre-school period, I am expected to assume a much larger role in the self-regulation of my impulses, even when I am not under direct adult supervision. I do continue to require some direction from my caregivers, drawing on my own resources first and seeking assistance when my efforts are exhausted or when special needs arise. Fantasy play is also a tool for emotional regulation at this time: I attribute make-believe feelings to my toys and to imaginary friends, which builds my capacity to appreciate and anticipate the emotional responses of others without actually experiencing them. Peer relationships are important, too: they foster an understanding of 'give-and-take' and, through them, I learn to be emotionally engaged, and to recognise and respond to the emotions of others.

My emotional skills are further honed during my school years when peer relationships become the primary venue for my emotional development. In the classroom, in the playground and on the sports field I learn that feelings and actions are different, that negative consequences will follow certain acts whilst positive consequences will follow others, and that I have a choice about how to respond to my impulses. With this awareness I learn the sophisticated arts of, for example, collaboration, conflict resolution, negotiation and compromise (which replace my former range of less complex reactions such as tantrums and outbursts); and the more I practise them, the more likely it is that I will have access to them in emotional crises. And so my emotional development unfolds, providing me with a larger and more nuanced repertoire of responses, and more and more ability to self-regulate when required, until I reach late adolescence (between sixteen and eighteen years of age) when my corticolimbic interfaces (the information pathways of the brain which connect the cortex to the amygdala in the limbic system) have matured, and

MINDS WITHOUT EMOTIONS ARE NOT REALLY
MINDS AT ALL. THEY ARE SOULS ON ICE –
COLD, LIFELESS CREATURES DEVOID
OF ANY DESIRES, FEARS, SOR-
ROWS, PAINS OR
PLEASURES.
LeDoux[52]

I am finally capable of independent functioning. My emotions emerged originally to prime me to act in emergency situations but, by my late teens, they are serving me in other ways, too. Feelings of attraction, love, and grief at loss enable me to communicate constructively my needs, intentions and desires, which is a vital achievement for all adult humans as members of a group-living, socially dependent species. My emotions are also motivating and organising – they guide, direct and fuel my behaviour, and so foster my productivity. They even facilitate the day-to-day decision-making upon which my modern life is built, signalling whom to trust or marry, which job to take, which house to buy and so on. And if I do achieve the happy position of being able to manage my emotions effectively, there is some evidence that I will not only lead a happier life, but a healthier and longer one, too.[53]

The above account describes the growth of a child who was fortunate to have emotionally intelligent caregivers who fostered his or her capacity for empathy and guided him or her through the emotional vicissitudes of childhood and adolescence. If we are not so fortunate – if we have parents who are emotionally immature – the challenge of progressing beyond *their* level of development can be onerous. And, as we all know (some of us too painfully), many children also suffer physical, sexual and/or mental abuse, or home lives which are highly stressed, or parents who are neglectful. Study after study has demonstrated that such trauma leaves a deep and lasting imprint on the developing brain[†] and, potentially, on the unfolding emotional competence of the young person concerned. Maladaptive responses (such as overwhelming anxiety, uncontrollable anger, hopelessness or guilt) may dominate and mould the limbic circuitry. The business of managing our emotions is difficult for all of us: we all experience what Goleman calls "emotional hijackings" from time to time. But, for those of us who have suffered trauma at vulnerable periods of our lives, the challenge is even greater. And how surmountable this challenge really is remains a focus of study and debate.

| TYPICAL ACHIEVEMENTS OF THE | |
|---|---|
| **EMOTIONAL STREAM** | |
| *Age / Stage* | *Principal emotional tasks* |
| Infancy<br>*Sensorimotor stage* | ❖ The expression of the basic emotions<br>❖ The expression of primitive forms of more complex emotions |
| Early childhood<br>*Impulsive stage* | ❖ Guided self-regulation of one's emotional responses |
| Middle to late childhood<br>*Imperial stage* | ❖ Increasing self-regulation of one's emotional responses |
| Adolescence<br>*Relational stage* | ❖ A large and nuanced repertoire of emotional responses |
| Young adulthood and beyond<br>*Organisational stage* | ❖ Independent functioning as a competent emotional being, i.e. the ability to:<br>• Recognise the specific feelings which trigger-stimuli arouse in oneself<br>• Understand those feelings – why the stimuli are emotionally arousing to oneself<br>• Control maladaptive bodily responses<br>• Select, consciously, appropriate responses to those stimuli |
| Mid-life and beyond<br>*World-Centric stage* | ❖ Continuous honing of one's emotional skills |

† *"The massive sculpting and pruning of neural circuits in childhood may be an underlying reason why early emotional hardships and trauma have such enduring and pervasive effects in adulthood. It may explain, too, why psychotherapy can often take so long to affect some of these patterns – and why... even after therapy those patterns tend to remain as underlying propensities, though with an overlay of new insights and relearned responses."*[54] *– Goleman*

SUMMARY *The Emotional stream describes the process of managing our responses to emotionally arousing stimuli. No comprehensive theory has yet been proposed to define how we become emotionally competent, but it is clear from the research of L. Alan Sroufe that this process is heavily influenced by the experiences of our early years. It is also clear from Joseph LeDoux's research that, at this point in our evolutionary history, the wiring of the human brain is such that the connections from the emotional systems to the cognitive systems are stronger than the connections from the cognitive systems to the emotional systems. Passions can and do flood consciousness even in the emotionally competent. But, based on trends in brain evolution, LeDoux has predicted that the struggle between thinking and feeling may ultimately be resolved as these nerve pathways may, over time, come into balance, providing for a more harmonious integration of reason and passion, which will enable future humans to know and use their emotions more effectively. In the meantime, however, the challenge of managing our emotions "with intelligence" can be nothing short of a life-long endeavour.*

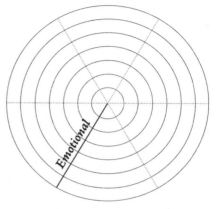

## II. e. *The Psychological Stream of development.*

he Psychological stream describes the process of forming an identity – our increasingly sophisticated way of perceiving ourselves, enabling us to orientate ourselves in the world. It follows the previous streams because our emerging sense of who we are integrates our achievements in these other domains. As this integration process is so complex and so influenced by personal experiences, it has been specified by the leading identity theorist, Jane Loevinger, as one of the primary dimensions of difference at all ages beyond infancy.

Loevinger notes that the subject of identity development has intrigued philosophers, and now psychologists, since at least the time of Socrates. (Socrates was the classical philosopher who, we learn in the *Dialogues* of Plato, called his followers to lead the "examined" life.) The following account is based on her sequence of ten levels of 'Ego Development' (1976), which she derived over many decades using what has proved to be a very robust 'Sentence Completion Test'.[55]

The sequence begins with the pre-social level, the now familiar post-birth period during which my main task is to achieve a differentiated Self. In the context of my primary caregiver relationships, I soon reach the symbiotic level where my ability to distinguish Self from non-Self is significantly advanced. With this knowledge of a distinct Self (a discovery which is facilitated by the development of language), I attain the impulsive level. Here, my impulses, curbed initially by caregiver constraint and, later, by immediate rewards and punishments, help me to affirm my separate identity, although my need for others is still, of course, strong and demanding and dependent (see the Impulsive stage).[56]

My movement towards the self-control of my impulses occurs when I learn to *anticipate* immediate short-term rewards and punishments. My controls are fragile at first and there is a vulnerability and guardedness in me, hence Loevinger's classification of this period as the self-protective level. I understand that there are rules now which I did not understand at the impulsive level and I use them, together with my understanding of cause and effect, to get what I want, with my main rule being "Don't get caught!" I have the notion of blame but I externalise it to other people and circumstances. Self-criticism is not characteristic.

Loevinger notes that a momentous step forward occurs in the development of my identity when I start to associate my welfare with that of my reference group (my family as a young child; my peer group as an older child). I am very invested in belonging to it, and obtaining its approval, because this makes me feel secure, and so I have now achieved the conformist level of the sequence. Interpersonally, I exhibit a superficial niceness, I obey the group-accepted rules, and if I break these rules I feel shame and guilt. I see the world in terms of external tangibles: I evaluate myself and others against criteria such as appearance, social acceptance, reputation and material things.

Loevinger concluded that the next position, the self-aware level[57], is the modal level of late adolescence and adult life in urban American society. An increase in self-awareness with a corresponding realisation that I do not always live up to the idealised portrait set by social norms, plus a recognition of multiple possibilities in situations, nudges me to this point, whereupon I begin to separate myself and what I want from my group and its rules. I have a growing appreciation of my relationship to other people as individuals (who are different from me and also from each other), and I have some experience of an inner life.

The next position is the conscientious level, which is rarely achieved before the age of fifteen. At this level, the major elements of an adult conscience are present in me, including long-term, self-determined goals and ideals, self-criticism, and a sense of responsibility and obligation, all of which imply a perception of 'choice', and that I see myself as the origin of my destiny. I have a rich inner life, and I aspire to achievement measured by my own standards, rather than by recognition or competitive advantage, as at lower levels.[58] Increasing conceptual sophistication is a hallmark, so I can think in terms of complex, differentiated polarities (such as trivial versus important, love versus lust, inner life versus outward appearances) and I have a longer-term perspective and a capacity to view events in a broader social context – characteristics which are even more salient at higher levels.

The next position, the individualistic level[59], is marked by a heightened sense of individuality: I now regard dependence on others when no longer physically or financially reliant as an emotional (rather than just a pragmatic) problem. I am, otherwise, more tolerant of myself and others – a toleration which grows out of the recognition of individual differences and the intricacies of circumstances that I achieved at the conscientious level. I have an awareness of inner conflict (although I will not know that such conflict is part of the human condition until I reach the next level). A further increase in conceptual sophistication enables me to work with complexity and paradox.[60]

At the next level, the autonomous level, I cherish my individuality. I also respect other people and their need for individuality, too, which may be expressed, for example, in a willingness to let my children make their own mistakes. I do, however, realise that autonomy has its limitations and that emotional interdependence is both necessary and precious to me, and so I express my feelings vividly and convincingly. The distinctive mark of this level is my new ability to acknowledge and cope with inner conflict – conflicting needs, conflicting duties, and the conflict between needs and duties. It is not that I have more conflict at this level than I had previously, but I have the courage to deal with it (I do not ignore it or project it onto my environment as I did at lower levels). At the conscientious level I saw the world in terms of polarities; at the autonomous level I partly transcend these polarities and see reality as compound and multifaceted. I am able to unite and integrate ideas which, formerly, would have appeared to me as incompatible alternatives, and I have a high threshold for ambiguity, uncertainty and flux.[61] Indeed, conceptual sophistication is an outstanding sign of this and the following level. I take a broad view of life as a whole, aspiring to be realistic and objective about myself and others for I recognise that we are all the product of our personal experiences. I am, therefore, interested in developing myself further, and self-fulfilment is now my goal, partly supplanting achievement.

The highest position is the integrated level, the new element of which is a consolidated sense of identity. Loevinger believed that the best description of it is the definition of 'self-actualisation' offered by the humanistic psychologist, Abraham H. Maslow.[62] Maslow defined self-actualisation as:

"...the full use and exploitation of talents, capacities, potentialities and the like. Such people seem to be fulfilling themselves and to be doing the best that they are capable of doing, reminding us of Nietzsche's exhortation, 'Become what thou art!' They are people who have developed or are developing to the full stature of which they are capable."[63]

From his research, Maslow identified a number of defining qualities of self-actualising people:

- They see reality more clearly (*what* is there rather than their own wishes, hopes, fears, anxieties, theories and beliefs, or those of their cultural group).
- They accept their own human nature with all its short-comings – *as it is* rather than how they would prefer it to be – with a relative lack of overriding guilt, shame or anxiety.
- They are relatively spontaneous in their behaviour and even more spontaneous in their inner life (with their thoughts, impulses and so on).
- They focus on problems outside themselves: they tend to have a non-personal, unselfish 'task that they must do' that they may or may not choose but they feel it to be their duty or obligation to fulfil.
- They like solitude and privacy to a greater degree than the average person; they are more detached and objective, and it is often possible for them to remain undisturbed by that which produces turmoil in others.

---

"MOST PEOPLE, AFTER ALL, DO NOT AMOUNT
TO MUCH BUT THEY COULD HAVE."
ABRAHAM H. MASLOW,[64]
citing one of his few self-
actualising subjects

---

+ They are autonomous: they make up their own minds, they
  come to their own decisions, they are self-starters and they
  are responsible for themselves and their own destinies, with
  or without the good opinion – or even the affection – of
  others.
+ They appreciate the basic, good things of life, however stale
  these experiences may become to others.
+ They have deep feelings of identity, sympathy and affection
  for human beings in general.
+ They are humble and respectful: they are able to learn from
  anybody who has something to teach them for they are well
  aware of how little they know in comparison with what
  could be known and what is known by others.
+ They have deeper, more profound interpersonal relations
  than other adults (necessarily, their circle of friends is small).
+ They have strong, ethical standards which are often unconventional.
+ They distinguish between, and enjoy, means and ends.
+ They have a sense of humour which is philosophical rather
  than hostile, eliciting a smile rather than a laugh.
+ They show a special kind of creativity or originality or
  inventiveness.
+ They resist enculturation, maintaining a certain inner
  detachment from the culture in which they are immersed.
+ They have imperfections (for, in Maslow's words, there are
  no perfect human beings and so, to avoid disillusionment
  with human nature, we must give up our illusions about it!).
+ They have a value system which arises from their philosophical acceptance of the nature of Self, of human nature,
  of much of social life, and of the natural world and physical
  reality.
+ They resolve the dichotomies, polarities or oppositions
  which dominate the thinking of those who are less mature.

This list of characteristics illustrates, comprehensively, Loevinger's assertion that the ego is the "central organizer". A self-actualising person has clearly achieved the highest level of sophistication in all the foregoing streams of development – the Intellectual, Social, Moral, and Emotional streams – as well as this, the Psychological stream. (Maslow also identified that some of his self-actualising subjects had what he called "peak experiences" – transformative moments of self-transcendent intensity – which prefigure, perhaps, the attainment of the highest level of the Spiritual stream.) Unsurprisingly, Maslow discovered that such self-actualising people are very few in number, and that those whom he could identify were always older, for younger people, he asserts, have not had the opportunity to meet the many preconditions that he believed apply:

"...youngsters have not yet achieved identity, or autonomy, nor have they had time enough to experience an enduring, loyal, post-romantic love relationship, nor have they generally found their calling, the altar upon which to offer themselves. Nor have they worked out their *own* system of values; nor have they had experience enough (responsibility for others, tragedy, failure, achievement, success) to shed perfectionistic illusions and become realistic; nor have they generally made their peace with death; nor have they learned how to be patient; nor have they learned enough about evil in themselves and others to be compassionate; nor have they had time to become post-ambivalent about parents and elders, power and authority; nor have they generally become knowledgeable and educated enough to open the possibility of becoming wise; nor have they generally acquired enough courage to be unpopular, to be unashamed about being openly virtuous etc."[65]

SUMMARY *The Psychological stream describes the process of forming an identity – an emerging sense of who we are which integrates our achievements in the*

TYPICAL ACHIEVEMENTS OF THE
# PSYCHOLOGICAL STREAM

| Age / Stage | Principal psychological tasks† |
|---|---|
| Infancy<br>*Sensorimotor stage* | ❖ A differentiated Self |
| Early childhood<br>*Impulsive stage* | ❖ The affirmation of a separate identity through the fulfilment of one's impulses |
| Middle to late childhood<br>*Imperial stage* | ❖ Increasing self-control of one's impulses<br>    *Then, if growth continues at this stage:*<br>❖ The identification of one's welfare with that of one's reference group<br>❖ Investment in one's reference group for security purposes<br>❖ The evaluation of Self and others on the basis of external tangibles |
| Adolescence<br>*Relational stage* | ❖ Increasing self-awareness<br>❖ A moving away from one's reference group<br>❖ An appreciation of relationships with others (who are different from Self and from each other)<br>❖ A sense of an inner life<br>    *Then, if growth continues at this stage:*<br>❖ Long-term, self-determined goals and ideals, self-criticism and a sense of responsibility and obligation<br>❖ A rich inner life<br>❖ An aspiration to achieve according to one's own standards     *(continued overleaf)* |

† *The important achievement of conceptual sophistication, which Jane Loevinger describes as an outstanding sign of the higher levels of identity development, is listed in the table of tasks associated with the Intellectual stream.*

---

# PSYCHOLOGICAL STREAM
*(cont'd)*

| | |
|---|---|
| Young adulthood and beyond *Organisational stage* | ❖ A heightened sense of individuality<br>❖ Tolerance of Self and others<br>❖ An awareness of inner conflict |
| Mid-life and beyond *World-Centric stage* | ❖ Respect for individuality (that of Self and others)<br>❖ Relationships of interdependence<br>❖ The ability to cope with inner conflict<br>❖ An interest in one's own development and a goal of self-fulfilment (partly supplanting achievement)<br>*Then, if growth continues at this stage:*<br>❖ A consolidated sense of identity – 'self-actualisation' |

preceding developmental streams, enabling us to orientate ourselves in the world. Jane Loevinger, who delineates identity (or the 'ego') as the "central organizer", mapped a sequence of ten levels of growth, noting that the modal adult achievement is a place of transition between the conformist position (where we measure ourselves by the standards of our reference group in which we are very invested) and the conscientious position (where we measure

ourselves by self-evaluated standards and see ourselves as the origin of our own destiny). At the highest position we become 'self-actualising' – a rare attainment indeed. Abraham Maslow remarks of those who have reached this level of maturation that they have so much to teach the rest of us that "they seem almost like a different breed of human beings".[66]

## II. f. The Spiritual stream of development.

he Spiritual stream describes the process of experiencing a transcendent dimension to human life. It follows the Psychological stream because the highest level of spiritual development is a *transpersonal* one. At this level, we have risen above the boundaries of the Self, a Self which achieved its fullest expression at the integrated, self-actualising position of the Psychological stream; and in this transpersonal state, according to the sages and mystics, the most profound insights become available to us.

The researcher and former nun, Karen Armstrong, who has completed a vast study of 4000 years of religion, notes in her book, *A History of God*, that we are, innately, spiritual animals who have always sought to understand the ultimate meaning of human life. For most of our history, of course, we have undertaken this search through the practices and observances of organised religions:

"…there is a case for arguing that *Homo sapiens* is also *Homo religiosus*. Men and women started to worship gods as soon as they become recognisably human; they created religions at the same time as they created works of art. This was not simply because they wanted to propitiate powerful forces but these early faiths expressed the wonder and mystery that seems always to have been an essential component of the human experience of this beautiful yet terrifying world. Like art, religion has been an attempt to find meaning and value in life, despite the suffering that flesh is heir to. Like any other human activity, religion can be abused but it seems to have been something that we have always done. It was not tacked on to a primordially secular nature by manipulative kings and priests but was natural to humanity."[67]

In 1981, James Fowler, a developmental psychologist who was a follower of Piaget, a colleague of Lawrence Kohlberg, and who was also ordained in the United Methodist Church, published a theory of spiritual development.[68] This theory consists of a sequence of six levels of 'faith' which, Fowler asserts, those who seek the possibility of transcendence (or 'Enlightenment' as it is often called) must, inevitably, follow. The term 'faith' does not necessarily denote a religious faith, and it is not to be equated with 'belief'. Instead, 'faith' describes a way of 'seeing': each level of 'faith' constitutes a world-view which is more encompassing than the previous one (see the reference in Chapter One to the Great Chain of Being, which is, of course, the historical representation of this model). Fowler's theory remains the most widely known and influential in the field, although several criticisms of it have been made.[69] These criticisms include the author's blurring of the distinctions between moral development, psychological development and spiritual development, and his use of the Judeo-Christian image of the biblical Kingdom of God to illustrate the highest level of the sequence, notwithstanding his declared intention to treat 'faith' as a generic (i.e. non-religious) human phenomenon. The following account of the Spiritual stream is, therefore, a simplified representation of Fowler's theory, modified with citations from Scott Peck and Ken Wilber where appropriate.

My infancy is described by Fowler as a period of undifferentiated faith during which the seeds of trust, courage, hope and love (qualities necessary for my later spiritual development) are nurtured in my caregiving relationship.[70] My transition to the first level of intuitive-projective faith begins, typically, by the age of two. Language is not well developed yet but I can organise my environment into mental pictures because my imagination is now a powerful and permanent force (see the Impulsive stage). Unrestrained and uninhibited by logical thought as I am at this age, I am very influenced by representations which awaken me to the domain of faith. (The danger of this vulnerable, fantasy-filled phase is that it can be exploited by witting or unwitting adults through the reinforcement of the taboos and doctrinal expectations of their particular religions. Such possession of my imagination by images of terror and destruction may well give rise to great fears that I will only be able to order and sort out when I am older and become capable of more reflective thinking.)[71]

My transition to the next level, mythic-literal faith, is precipitated by the emergence of concrete operational thinking, my growing concern to know how things are, to sort out the real from the make-believe (see the Intellectual stream). I will now insist on a demonstration of proof for claims of fact for, as a ten-year-old, I am, in Fowler's words, a "young empiricist". I do not cease to be imaginative, but I submit the products of my imagination to more logical forms of scrutiny before I admit them as part of what I 'know'. I live, therefore, in "a more predictable and patterned – if more prosaic – world". At this level, a new ability emerges to bind my experiences into meaning through the medium of story. This interest in narrative makes me very attentive to cosmic accounts which conserve the origins and formative experiences of my particular reference group. I then take on for myself the beliefs and observances which symbolise my belonging to this group.[72]

My transition to the third level of spiritual development, synthetic-conventional faith, has its rise during my adolescence (and, for a considerable number of adults, this is their permanent place of equilibrium). It is precipitated by the emergence of formal operational thinking – the capacity to reflect upon myself, my experiences and my thinking (see the Intellectual stream). But my personal philosophy at this level is not the result of a genuine introspective process. I am still very reliant on external authority and my thinking is therefore 'conventional' or 'synthetic' in that it is non-analytical. I am aware of having an ideology, a more-or-less consistent clustering of beliefs which provides me with a coherent orientation in the midst of a more complex and diverse range of involvements (with family, school or work, peers, street society, the media and, perhaps, religion). I articulate that ideology, defend it, and feel a deep emotional investment in it. But I have not made it the object of my reflection: it is my means of asserting my solidarity with my community rather than an independent perspective. If God remains, or becomes salient to me, that God undergoes a recomposition, for my hunger as an adolescent is for a God who knows, accepts and confirms my Self deeply (see the Relational stage, a stage at which I only know myself through my relationships). And so the images of transcendence which appeal to me now have the qualities of companionship, guidance, support, and of knowing and loving me, enabling me to have a more intimate connection with that ultimate power.[73]

My transition to the fourth level, individuative-reflective faith, represents an upheaval in my life for it occurs when I encounter experiences or perspectives which lead to critical reflection on how my beliefs have formed, and on how 'relative' they are to my particular group or culture. The experience of leaving home may, for example, be the catalyst for this examination of my world-view because it allows me to extract myself from the context in which it was largely formed, maintained and limited. Alternatively, the transition, if it comes at all, may not occur until I am in my thirties or forties, triggered perhaps by a significant life change – such as divorce, the death of a parent, children growing up and leaving home, moving house or changing jobs. To make this transition I must cease to be reliant on external sources of authority and relocate that authority within my Self. Now I have a world-view which I form and reform over time and which is differentiated from that of others. This is also a period of demythologising[74]: I interrogate dispassionately the symbols and rituals that I previously assumed mediated the sacred and were, therefore, sacred themselves.[75]

An awareness, which is unusual before middle age, that life is more complex than individuative-reflective faith's logic of clear distinctions and abstract concepts, will press me to the fifth level, conjunctive faith. Now I see both (or the many) sides of an issue simultaneously, and I can attend to the pattern of interrelatedness amongst things. Consequently, I am ready for significant encounters with other traditions, expecting that truth discloses itself to these traditions in ways which complement or correct my own. At this level, I cannot live with the demythologising strategy of individuative-reflective faith. I can appreciate again symbols and rituals (those of my own truth tradition and those of others) because I have been grasped in some measure by the depth of reality to which they refer. I can also see the rifts in the human family vividly because I have apprehended the possibility of an inclusive community of being. But at this level, I live and act in a divided state, between an untransformed world and a transforming vision. Paralysing passivity and inaction, giving rise to complacency or cynical withdrawal, may be the outcome of my paradoxical understanding of the truth. It is very unlikely indeed that I will resolve this conflict within me by moving on to the next level of growth.[76]

This rare and final position is the level of universalising faith, which corresponds to the Self-Transcendent stage described in Chapter One (so the ultimate expression of the Spiritual stream is the Self-Transcendent stage of development). At this level, I live in the transforming vision I glimpsed at the conjunctive level of faith.[77] My mind has, in the words of Wilber, "expanded to include the All": I have separated from my thinking (i.e. my own thoughts and ideas), from my relationships, from my moral perspective, from my emotions and from my identity. So I have transcended the boundaries of the Self that I have worked so hard to formulate since I was an infant. I have now become the 'Observing Self' or the 'Witness'. And as the 'Witness' (a state which might be perceived, erroneously, by others as one of non-compassion because, when I achieve it, I am liberated from all the suffering and terror which prevail in the world as a place of disparate objects), I discover that 'reality' is 'oneness'. To cite Peck again: "... our common perception of the universe as containing multitudes of discrete objects — stars, planets, trees, birds, houses, ourselves

– all separated from one another by boundaries is a misperception, an illusion."[78]

This level of awareness ("Kosmic[79] Consciousness" in Wilber's words) is the domain of the sages and the mystics, and those who have achieved it even attest to there being many sublevels within it. Wilber notes that current research indicates that at least four such sublevels exist (the Psychic, the Subtle, the Causal and the Non-Dual[80]) and that the very few "daring men and women" who have made this interior journey to self-transcendence have left their maps of the way so that those who have not may follow:

"In looking at these higher stages or waves of consciousness, we have a rather small pool of daring men and women – both yesterday and today – who have bucked the system, fought the average and normal, and struck out toward the new and higher spheres of awareness. In this quest, they joined with a small group, or *sangha*, of like-spirited souls, and developed *practices* or *injunctions* or *paradigms* that would disclose these higher worldspaces – injunctions or paradigms or interior *experiments* that would allow others to reproduce their results and therefore check and validate (or reject) their findings. And they left us their maps of this interior journey, with the crucial proviso that memorising the map will not do, any more than studying a map of the Bahamas will replace actually going there."[81]

Numbered amongst these sages and mystics are, of course, the prophets of the world's great religions, and it is their maps which inform the observances of these traditions. But maps to the higher reaches of spiritual development are available to the non-religious too, as Armstrong explains:

"Humanism is itself a religion without God – not all religions, of course, are theistic. Our ethical secular ideal has its own disciplines of mind and heart and gives people the means of finding faith in the ultimate meaning of human life that were once provided by the more conventional religions."[82]

The insights revealed to us at this level of universalising faith may be profound but all the theorists are agreed that very few

TYPICAL ACHIEVEMENTS OF THE

# SPIRITUAL STREAM

| Age / Stage | Principal spiritual tasks |
| --- | --- |
| Infancy<br>*Sensorimotor stage* | ❖ The establishment of the seeds of trust, courage, hope, and love (required for spiritual development) |
| Early childhood<br>*Impulsive stage* | ❖ The organisation of one's experiences into mental pictures |
| Middle to late childhood<br>*Imperial stage* | ❖ The sorting of the real from the make-believe<br>❖ The binding of one's experiences into meaning through narrative<br>❖ The adoption of the beliefs and observances of one's reference group |
| Adolescence<br>*Relational stage* | ❖ A conventional personal philosophy<br>❖ If an ultimate power remains, that God is a personal and loving God |
| Young adulthood and beyond<br>*Organisational stage* | ❖ The realisation that one's beliefs are 'relative' to one's reference group or culture<br>❖ A relocation of authority within the Self<br>❖ A personal world-view which forms and reforms over time<br>❖ Critical interrogation of symbols and rituals previously held as sacred |
| Mid-life and beyond<br>*World-Centric stage* | ❖ Significant encounters with other truth traditions<br>❖ Renewed appreciation of those symbols and rituals which are the expression of disclosed truth<br>❖ The awareness of humanity as an inclusive community of being |
| Maturity<br>*Self-Transcendent stage* | ❖ The capacity to transcend the boundaries of the Self |

of us, whether we are religious or non-religious, ever experience them, because the practices of self-transcendence require an extraordinary commitment and discipline. As Wilber asserts, "memorising the map will not do". Certainly, Fowler struggled to find anyone in the course of his research who had achieved this level of his developmental sequence.

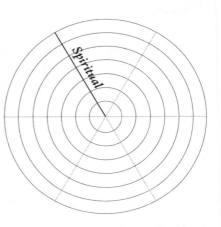

SUMMARY *The Spiritual stream describes the process of experiencing a transcendent dimension to human life. James Fowler identified a sequence of six levels of spiritual development, the highest of which is a transpersonal level where the Self gives up the ego boundaries it has crafted so carefully over the years, and discovers the unity of the universe, the ultimate reality of oneness. This position is also the final stage of the human development journey, the realm of the sages and mystics, and a very, very rare accomplishment indeed. For many, of course, to follow this particular stretch of pathway towards what is often called 'Enlightenment', is the pursuit of unreason. As the author, I leave the last word on this matter to Ken Wilber, who asks this question of anyone with a materialistic world-view who is, nevertheless, willing to interrogate his or her own thinking:*

*"Are the mystics and sages insane? Because they all tell variations on this same story, don't they? The story of awakening one morning and discovering that you are one with the All, in a timeless and eternal and infinite fashion.*

*"Yes, maybe they are crazy, these divine fools. Maybe they are mumbling idiots in the face of the Abyss...*

*"But then I wonder... in the highest reaches of evolution, maybe, just maybe, an individual's consciousness does indeed touch infinity – a total embrace of the entire Kosmos – a Kosmic consciousness that is Spirit awakened to its own nature.*

*"It's at least plausible. And tell me: is that story, sung by mystics and sages the world over, any crazier than the scientific materialism story, which is that the entire sequence is a tale told by an idiot, full of sound and fury, signifying absolutely nothing? Listen very carefully: just which of those two stories actually sounds totally insane?"*[83]

### *III. Conclusion.*

n Chapter One we explored the stages of the universal development journey. In this chapter we have explored some of the streams of development which flow through the basic stages – the challenges which present in the Intellectual, Social, Moral, Emotional, Psychological and Spiritual domains, all of which we must overcome if we are to progress to the next stage of our journey as a fully integrated Self. Our Intellectual development is fundamental to the whole course of our growth: if we cannot achieve Jean Piaget's level of formal operations, the capacity to reflect upon ourselves, our experiences and our thinking, our progress through all the streams will be severely limited. Similarly, our achievements in the Social stream, particularly our ability to take the role of 'the other', are foundational, too. And it is through our progress along the Psychological stream that we integrate *all* our accomplishments for, in the words of Jane Loevinger, our identity is the "central organizer". Finally, the opportunity for spiritual development is available to us through the Spiritual stream, which culminates at a transpersonal level where, according to those who have achieved this extraordinary state of self-transcendence, the most profound insights of human experience are revealed.†

These manifold challenges have been the subject of study of philosophers of the past, and developmental psychologists of the present, and we now have an increasingly sophisticated set of maps to guide us on our journey.

† *As the literary critic, Jill Mann, observes, the knights who are least successful in the Grail quest are not those who fail in their adventures. They are those who simply do not have any. In one of Thomas Malory's French sources for* Le Morte Darthur, *King Pelinore explains to King Arthur why he hunts the Questing Beast: "...because I wanted to know for a truth whether I was the best of our lineage, I have pursued it for so long. And I haven't said this to exalt myself, but to know the truth about myself."*[84]

| | Intellectual stream | Social stream | Moral stream |
|---|---|---|---|
| **Sensorimotor stage** *Infancy* | • The awareness of 'Self' <br> • The construction of object permanence | • An awareness of 'the other' <br> • Secure attachments to specific individuals | |
| **Impulsive stage** *Early childhood* | • Magical thought processes | • Early socialisation | • The definition of an action as 'right' or 'wrong' according to whether or not it is consistent with the rules, and whether or not punishment will follow |
| **Imperial stage** *Middle to late childhood* | • Logical thought processes | • Pro-social behaviour | • The definition of an action as 'right' or 'wrong' according to whether or not it serves one's own needs |
| **Relational stage** *Adolescence* | • Abstract thought processes, i.e. the capacity to reflect upon Self, one's experiences and one's thinking (one's own thoughts and ideas) | • Interpersonal relationships | • The definition of an action as 'right' or 'wrong' according to whether or not it pleases or helps others, and is approve by them |
| **Organisational stage** *Young adulthood and beyond* | • An increasing capacity for conceptual thinking | • Social competence (i.e. the ability to relate to, adapt to, and function with, other people) | • The definition of an action as 'right' or 'wrong' according to whether or not it maintains the given social order |
| **World-Centric stage** *Mid-life and beyond* | • Conceptual sophistication (enabling oneself, for example, to engage in subjective, interpersonal and non-rational thought processes, and to embrace complexity, paradox, ambiguity, uncertainty and flux) <br> — <br> • The capacity to participate in group thinking | • Continuous honing of one's social skills | • The definition of an action as 'right' or 'wrong' according to whether or not it makes for a good society (this requir a recognition that one's own reference group's definition of 'right' and 'wrong' is only one among many, plus a preparedness to make distinctions about which ethical principles are the most conducive to the development of humankind) <br> — <br> • Self-chosen ethical principles and a pr paredness to take action to defend the |
| **Self-Transcendent stage** *Maturity* | • The capacity to separate Self from one's own thinking | • The capacity to separate Self from one's own relationships | • The capacity to separate Self from one's own moral position |

| Emotional stream | Psychological stream | Spiritual stream |
|---|---|---|
| + The expression of the basic emotions<br>+ The expression of primitive forms of more complex emotions | + A differentiated Self | + The establishment of the seeds of trust, courage, hope, and love (required for spiritual development) |
| + Guided self-regulation of one's emotional responses | + The affirmation of a separate identity through the fulfilment of one's impulses | + The organisation of one's experiences into mental pictures |
| + Increasing self-regulation of one's emotional responses | + Increasing self-control of one's impulses<br>—<br>+ The identification of one's welfare with that of one's reference group<br>+ Investment in one's reference group for security purposes<br>+ The evaluation of Self and others on the basis of external tangibles | + The sorting of the real from the make-believe<br>+ The binding of one's experiences into meaning through narrative<br>+ The adoption of the beliefs and observances of one's reference group |
| + A large and nuanced repertoire of emotional responses | + Increasing self-awareness<br>+ A moving away from one's reference group<br>+ An appreciation of relationships with others (who are different from Self and from each other)<br>+ A sense of an inner life<br>—<br>+ Long-term, self-determined goals and ideals, self-criticism and a sense of responsibility and obligation<br>+ A rich inner life<br>+ An aspiration to achieve according to one's own standards | + A conventional personal philosophy<br>+ If an ultimate power remains, that God is a personal and loving God |
| + Independent functioning as a competent emotional being, i.e. the ability to:<br>· Recognise the specific feelings that trigger-stimuli arouse in oneself<br>· Understand those feelings – why the stimuli are emotionally arousing to oneself<br>· Control maladaptive bodily responses<br>· Select, consciously, appropriate responses to those stimuli | + A heightened sense of individuality<br>+ Tolerance of Self and others<br>+ An awareness of inner conflict | + The realisation that one's beliefs are 'relative' to one's reference group or culture<br>+ A relocation of authority within the Self<br>+ A personal world-view which forms and reforms over time<br>+ Critical interrogation of symbols and rituals previously held as sacred |
| + Continuous honing of one's emotional skills | + Respect for individuality (that of Self and others)<br>+ Relationships of interdependence<br>+ The ability to cope with inner conflict<br>+ An interest in one's own development and a goal of self-fulfilment (partly supplanting achievement)<br>—<br>+ A consolidated sense of identity: 'self-actualisation' | + Significant encounters with other truth traditions<br>+ Renewed appreciation of those symbols and rituals which are the expression of disclosed truth<br>+ The awareness of humanity as an inclusive community of being |
| + The capacity to separate Self from ones' own emotional responses | + The capacity to separate Self from one's own identity | + The capacity to transcend the boundaries of the Self |

Maps there are aplenty, then, but the *approach* we should take
to address the challenges we face cannot be defined by the theorists or, indeed, by the mystics, because it will, inevitably, be influenced by our own, individual personality. This is the matter of
Chapter Three but, before we move on, we can summarise Chapter Two with some additions to our rules of the road:

### The rules of the road.

1. The human development journey begins in infancy and, if growth
   continues, may extend into late adulthood and even until death
   (some, of course, may say that it extends beyond death).
2. The path that we, as travellers, follow is one of many distinct
   stages, each of which represents a clear, qualitative transformation of thinking and being.
3. The strengths of one stage ultimately become its limitations, a
   realisation which nudges us to the next stage of our growth.
4. We progress from one stage to the next by the agency of two fundamental capacities: transcendence and inclusion.
5. Research has consistently demonstrated that these stages cannot
   be bypassed without some compromise.
6. Each stage of the journey offers a new set of challenges (intellectual, social, moral, emotional, psychological and even spiritual
   challenges) which flow as streams of development through the
   basic stages of development.
7. These streams unfold as the stages unfold, by the same agencies
   of transcendence and inclusion, and also with their own dynamic.
8. If, in our determination to press onwards, we choose not to confront all the challenges available to us in the streams of development, we will arrive at the next stage of our development with
   some of our potential unrealised, with an imbalance in our sphere
   of total capability.
9. To function as a fully integrated Self, therefore, we must recognise our development gaps and then seek out those stream-specific learning experiences which will enable us to attend to them.

# FINDING
# MERLIN

*CHAPTER THREE*

# THE
# *KNIGHT*
# ADVENTUROUS

*Now rideth Galahad yet without shield, and so rode four days without any adventure. And at the fourth day after evensong he came to a white abbey and there was he received with great reverence and led unto a chamber, and there was he unarmed. And then was he ware of two knights of the Table Round, one was Sir Bagdemagus, and Sir Uwain. [...]*

*So on the morn they arose and heard Mass; then King Bagdemagus asked where the adventurous shield was. Anon a monk led him behind an altar where the shield hung, as white as any snow, but in the midst was a red cross.*

*"Sirs," said the monk, "this shield ought not to be hung about the neck of no knight but he be the worthiest knight of the world: therefore I counsel you, knights, to be well advised."*

*"Well," said Sir Bagdemagus, "I wot well I am not the best knight, but I shall assay to bear it"; and so bore it out of the monastery... and then they saw a knight... in white armour, horse and all, and he came as fast as his horse might run, and his spear in his rest. Then Sir Bagdemagus dressed his spear against him and broke it upon the white knight; but the other struck him so hard that he brast the mails and thrust him through the right shoulder, for the shield covered him not as at that time. And so he bore him from his horse; and therewith he alit and took his white shield from him, saying, "Knight, thou hast done thyself great folly, for this shield ought not to be borne but by him that shall have no peer that liveth." And then he came to Bagdemagus' squire and bade him, "Bear this shield to the good knight Sir Galahad that thou left in the abbey, and greet him well by me."*[1]

The Tale of the Sangrail, of Sir Galahad

LE MORTE DARTHUR

Thomas Malory

❖　❖

❖

# The Knight Adventurous

hapter Two described the many challenges we encounter as we make our way along the human development road – the intellectual, social, moral, emotional, psychological and spiritual challenges that we must address on the path to becoming a fully integrated Self. Universally applicable they may be, but the way in which we address them will differ from individual to individual because our own personality has a significant influence on our behaviour.

## I. What is this thing called 'personality'?

e all use the term 'personality' in our everyday language to describe one person to another. We regularly employ simple words such as 'quiet', 'reserved', 'jovial', 'energetic' or 'forthright' to codify a multifarious set of characteristics. However, anyone who has been on a blind date with someone who was reported to have a 'nice' personality will know how uninformative these descriptors can be! And we are usually offended at being so easily pigeonholed ourselves. We know that we are more complex than these labels suggest, that we react differently to different sets of variables, and that we can be flexible in our responses, too, if we need to be.

So we all have some notion of what 'personality' is but, like 'intelligence', it has proved to be notoriously difficult to define theoretically; psychologists, from their own viewpoints, have delineated it in many different ways. Happily, the scholars, Tony Malim and Anne Birch, report that I.L. Child's definition is accepted by many: it is the "more or less stable, internal factors that make one person's behaviour consistent from one time to another, and different from the behaviour other people would manifest in comparable situations" (1968).[2][†] This is a definition, therefore, which includes the notions of consistency (within the individual) and difference (between individuals), and indicates that it is our personality which causes our behaviour to be (relatively) consistent, and which also causes each of us to behave differently from each other. We acknowledge these notions of consistency and difference in our conversations. Phrases such as "That's just like John", or "I know already how Julie will react to this", illustrate our intuitive understanding of those in our acquaintance. When we refer to others as 'moody' or 'persistent' or 'fussy' or 'laid-back' we are not only referring to their outward expression in the moment. We are describing a pattern of responses that we have observed over time and which characterise them. And just as we make assumptions about how others will address the particular challenges which confront them, they also make such assumptions about us!

This subject of intra-individual coherence ('true-to-self') and inter-individual differentiation ('diversity') has been a source of fascination since earliest times. The physician, Hippocrates (460–377 BCE), assigned people to one of four types of temperament (Sanguine, Phlegmatic, Melancholic and Choleric) on the basis of a predominance of body fluids (blood, phlegm, black bile and yellow bile), and these terms are still used occasionally today to describe personality.

† PERSONALITY VS TEMPERAMENT VS CHARACTER *Within psychology two classic definitions of personality are used – I.L. Child's, as described above, and Gordon Allport's: "Personality is the dynamic organization within the individual of psychophysical systems that determine his characteristic behavior and thought" (1961). 'Temperament' is assumed to be the biological soil from which personality develops. 'Character' is assumed to be personality evaluated within a social, cultural and moral framework. So, to use a gardening metaphor, personality is rooted in the biological soil and evaluated in the social, cultural and moral climate.*

*The armorial bearings of Sir Lancelot.*

he heraldic scholar, Gerard Brault, describes how Sir Lancelot (who would have been the greatest of all the knights of the Company of the Round Table but for his adulterous love for King Arthur's queen) acquired his traditional bearings.[3]

In his early adventures in the great thirteenth-century French *Vulgate Cycle* of romances, he wears the white armour given to him by the Lady of the Lake. Later, how-  ever, as he prepares to capture the castle of Dolorous Guard, he receives three enchanted shields from her. All are white, but the first, which has the power to impart to its owner the strength of one man, has a single red 'bend' (a wide, oblique band); the second has two red bends representing the strength of two men; and the third has three red bends for the strength of three men. Aided by these shields and in particular, of course, the third, he overcomes in combat all the knights who are defending the castle, and so he is able to capture it.

Thereafter, Brault notes, Lancelot's shield in Old French literature and medieval art is usually blazoned 'argent, three bends gules'. So the field of the shield is 'argent', which is elevated language for the colour white or silver, and a colour which signifies peace and sincerity in medieval heraldry. The central charges are three bends: a bend signifies defence or protection, and the bearing of objects in threes signifies the Trinity (the union of the Father, the Son and the Holy Spirit in one Godhead in Christian doctrine). And the colour of the bends is 'gules' (red) which signifies military fortitude and magnanimity.[4]

In the *Vulgate Cycle*, which was an important source for Sir Thomas Malory's *Le Morte Darthur*, the revelation of Lancelot's sexual sin precipitates the fall of the Round Table, and is the central moral lesson of this text. Malory, however, departs from his French source in his emphasis upon how close Lancelot comes to achieving the Grail (rather than upon his failure).[5] With his physical prowess and his commitment to the terms of the oath of the Round Table, he is the paragon of earthly knighthood. He is faithful to Queen Guenivere whom he cannot renounce; he is faithful to King Arthur as his lord; and he is faithful to the chivalric brotherhood which he wants to restore. Malory's narrative may be more a chronicle of events than a study of individualised characters, but we experience enough consistency in his portrayal of Lancelot to be able to accord him his traditional bearings and also to recognise him fully in the moving threnody which his brother, Sir Ector, offers over his dead body at the conclusion of this great story:

*Ah, Lancelot… thou were head of all Christian knights! And now*
*I dare say… thou, Sir Lancelot, there thou liest, that thou were*
*never matched of earthly knight's hand. And thou were the*
*courteoust knight that ever bore shield: and thou were the*
*truest friend to thy lover that ever bestrode horse; and*
*thou were the kindest man that ever struck with*
*sword; and thou were the goodliest person*
*that ever came among press of knights.*
*And thou was the meekest man and*
*the gentlest that ever ate in hall*
*among ladies, & thou were*
*the sternest knight to thy*
*mortal foe that ever*
*put spear in*
*the rest.*

✤

In the medieval period, personality was signified in the armorial bearings of the battlefield. As the heraldic scholar, Oswald Barron, remarks, one galloping knight would have looked much the same as another, and so self-assumed blazonry was employed for identification purposes.[6] Knights selected colours and devices which symbolised the personal characteristics that they believed (or hoped!) distinguished them. And, if they wanted to be anonymous, they bore shields of plain colours without devices – which is why the white knight, in the extract from *Le Morte Darthur* above, remains unknown.

Then, in the sixteenth century, the Italian theatre form, Commedia dell'arte, articulated this fascination with personality in its system of masks, which were used not to *disguise* the identity of the characters but to *typify* them in terms of their behaviour. In fact, the word 'personality' derives, at least in part, from the Late Latin word *persona*, which means 'mask'.

THE MASK OF HARLEQUIN
*In the Commedia dell'arte system of masks, certain physical features of the masks are associated with certain internal characteristics. Harlequin's colourful, patched costume and black, bulging face covering, for example, denote a figure who is simple, naive, easily confused, very agile and always hungry – for both food and love!*

Modern psychologists are equally fascinated by the elusive phenomenon of personality. As noted above, they have offered different definitions of it. They have also advanced many and various (and often contradictory) theories to describe the psychological processes of which it is composed. Two of the most commonly referenced approaches are those of 'trait' and 'type':

*Trait approaches to personality.* Traits are defined as the stable and enduring aspects of personality which are thought to be normally distributed throughout the population and therefore possessed by everyone, but to varying degrees. Much of the recent research in personality has centred on the concept of trait rather than the concept of type, and both single-trait theories (which emphasise the role played by a particular aspect of personality in influencing behaviour) and multi-trait theories (which attempt to describe the whole personality) have been developed by theorists to explain it.[7] Traits are represented as paired oppositions – examples from our everyday language might include 'open' versus 'closed', 'aggressive' versus 'passive', 'creative' versus 'conservative', and so on.

*Type approaches to personality.* Some theorists subscribe to the view that individuals may be categorised into distinct personality types. (Hippocrates's typology is probably the earliest recorded example of type theory.) Types differ from traits in that a person cannot be said to possess a type to a varying degree: the person either is or is not categorised as a specific type.[8] An example from our everyday language would be the 'strong, silent type'.

So the term 'personality' defies a single definition, and there is no agreement amongst researchers about the psychological processes of which it is composed. Further questions also arise when we examine this subject closely.[9] What, for example, actually determines behaviour consistencies? Which, if any, have a genetic basis and are, therefore, inherited? Which, if any, are socially constructed and are, therefore, learned responses? Biological and social learning theories have been proposed to address these questions; they have their advocates and their critics, and add to the mix of theoretical approaches described above. Then there is the long-standing question of how the situation confronting an individual influences his or her behaviour, which was explored by the psychologist, Viktor Frankl, in his vivid account of his struggle for survival in the hunger, cold and brutality of Auschwitz and other Nazi concentration camps (*Man's Search for Meaning*). Academic research has demonstrated that the situation can, indeed, have a compelling effect on behaviour, and situationist approaches have therefore been developed to accommodate this. Again, they have their advocates and their critics, and so interactionist approaches have now been presented which incorporate internal characteristics of people and features of the situations in which they operate, *and also* the process by which one influences the other. These interactionist approaches have their supporters and detractors, too, adding still further to the complexity of the field. And, finally, there is the question of how consistent personality is over time. Kevin Durkin observes that personality has been described by Gordon Allport as a "dynamic organization", a description which offers the possibility that it is *continuously* open to change, as, for example, we encounter new experiences and adapt to them.[10]

Notwithstanding all this complexity, however, we, in our daily activities of meeting, talking, working and playing with each other, acquire an understanding of this phenomenon called 'personality'. We know that it affects how we respond to other people; how we see the world (because it serves as a self-formed lens which draws some things into focus and pushes some things into the distance); how we solve problems; and how we choose to live our lives.[11]

### II. Lenses on personality.

he theoretical disputes about the nature of personality continue but, in the meantime, an assortment of models and instruments have been formulated which enable responders to explore their own behavioural consistencies. These devices are widely used in organisations today for individual and team development purposes, and include the Five Factor Model (a trait approach to personality assessment) and the Myers-Briggs Type Indicator (a type approach to personality assessment).

### *II. a. The Five Factor Model.*[12]

his model describes a hierarchical organisation of personality traits in terms of five broad domains which, its advocates claim, form the basis of personality structure. These domains emerged over several decades of study by a number of independent researchers using various methods on samples of children and adults across many cultures. It is founded on two traditions rather than a particular theory of personality:

1. The lexical hypothesis, which holds that all important individual differences will have been noted by speakers of a natural language at some point in its evolution and encoded in trait terms (and so, by decoding them, we can discover the basic dimensions of personality).

2. The analysis of a wide range of personality questionnaires with scales designed for specific practical applications or to measure constructs derived from personality theory.

The domains were first 'announced' in 1961 in a US Air Force report produced by Ernest Tupes and Raymond Christal. They had factor-analysed personality data using trait measures which another researcher, Raymond Cattell, had identified from an original listing created in 1936 (by Gordon Allport and H.S. Odbert) of almost 18,000 trait names gathered from English-language dictionaries. Tupes and Christal's analysis revealed, to their surprise, five recurring common factors: Extraversion, Agreeableness, Conscientiousness, Neuroticism and Culture. Their results were then replicated by Warren Norman in 1963.

The importance of these factors remained hidden from most personality psychologists throughout the 1960s and 1970s. In the 1980s, however, researchers from many traditions rediscovered them and concluded that they were, indeed, fundamental dimensions of personality. In 1985, Robert McCrae and Paul Costa proposed that Culture should be reconceptualised as Openness to

Experience. Most current researchers agree with them and so we now have a classification of personality attributes as follows:

- Extraversion (versus Introversion)
- Agreeableness (versus Disagreeableness)
- Conscientiousness (versus Lack of Conscientiousness)
- Neuroticism (versus Emotional Stability)
- Openness to Experience (versus Closedness to Experience)

McCrae and Costa have also identified specific sets of six facets which they list as the constituents of the five factors:

*Extraversion:*
- Warmth
- Gregariousness
- Assertiveness
- Activity
- Excitement-seeking
- Positive emotions

*Agreeableness:*
- Trust
- Straightforwardness
- Altruism
- Compliance
- Modesty
- Tender-mindedness

*Conscientiousness:*
- Competence
- Order
- Dutifulness
- Achievement-striving
- Self-discipline
- Deliberation

*Neuroticism:*
- Anxiety
- Hostility
- Depression
- Self-consciousness
- Impulsiveness
- Vulnerability

*Openness to Experience:*
- Fantasy
- Aesthetics
- Feelings
- Actions
- Ideas
- Values

Subsequent research has provided substantial evidence of the universality of the factors, and of the heritability of many of them (which indicates a strong genetic component to them). Longitudinal investigations have also indicated a high degree of stability for them from early adulthood onwards.[13]

The model does have its critics. Some psychologists have suggested that the five factors can be reduced to three, or even to two, higher-order factors. Other psychologists have suggested that there are some additional fundamental dimensions of personality which are not included in the 'Big Five'. (Amongst them is Catell, whose work, as noted above, informed the study method of the US Air Force analysts who first identified the 'Big Five'. His own, competing, approach, represented in the '16PF' questionnaire, has been designed to assess the structure of personality using a sixteen-factor solution.)

Even its most ardent supporters would not argue that the five factors provide a *complete* description of personality. As McCrae himself and his co-writer, Oliver P. John, note, the model cannot account for all the richness of human individuality.[14] And, as a multi-trait approach which organises personality at a high level, it is certainly not as effective at predicting *actual* behaviour as single-trait approaches (such as Rotter's 'Internal-External Locus of Control' theory, McClelland et al's 'Need for Achievement' theory or Friedman and Rosenham's 'Type A Personality' theory). Neither does it explain the dynamic operation of traits in our everyday lives. Nevertheless, the model and the various instruments and questionnaires which have been formulated to apply it (including the 'Revised NEO Personality Inventory' developed by McCrae and Costa) remain very popular with psychologists as a methodology for understanding and measuring personality in respondents and, therefore, for predicting characteristic patterns of behaviour.†

† *"In addition to the empirical evidence for the model, there is something intuitively appealing about the factors: they make a great deal of sense. In part, this may be because they make explicit the implicit personality theory that is encoded in the personality language we all use; in part, the model probably squares well with our experience of self and others." – McCrae and John*[15]

## II. b. The Myers-Briggs Type Indicator.[16]

he MBTI instrument is based on Carl Jung's theory of psychological type. Jung was a psychiatrist who, from his observations over fifty years during the last century, asserted that there are predictable and differing patterns of normal human behaviour which are caused by the differences in the way that people innately prefer to use their minds. Then a mother-and-daughter pair, Katherine Cook Briggs and Isabel Myers, who were also keen and disciplined observers of personality differences, worked on Jung's ideas and devised an assessment tool to give individuals access to the benefits of knowing their personality type.

There are two components to Jung's picture of personality:

1. *Orientation of energy*: Jung's initial attention to personality differences stemmed from his recognition that there are two types of people: extroverts and introverts.[17] Extroverts tend to direct their energy towards, and be energised more by, the external world of other people, experience and activity; introverts tend to direct their energy towards, and be more energised by, the internal world of ideas, memories and emotions.

2. *The basic mental processes*: Jung also observed that when our minds are active, they are involved in one of two mental exercises: taking in information (which he called 'perceiving') and organising that information and coming to conclusions ('judging'). He also identified two opposite ways in which we perceive, which he called 'sensation' and 'intuition', and two opposite ways in which we judge, which he called 'thinking' and 'feeling'. In his book, *Psychological Types*, he described these four processes in great detail but summarised the information very succinctly thus in *Man and His Symbols*, published posthumously in 1964:

"These four function[s]… correspond to the obvious means by which consciousness obtains its orientation to experience. *Sensation* (i.e. sense perception) tells you that something exists; *thinking* tells you what it is; *feeling* tells you whether it is agreeable or not; and *intuition* tells you whence it comes and where it is going."[18]

Each of these four basic mental processes has its own predictable characteristics and, in all of us, one of these processes (either sensing, intuition, thinking or feeling) will be used most enthusiastically, most often and with the greatest confidence, and is, therefore, our 'dominant function'. This dominant function, Jung believed, effectively directs or 'dominates' our personality.

Jung then specified which of the two orientations of extraversion and introversion is likely to be used habitually in conjunction with our dominant mental function, leading us to direct our energy towards it and to develop habits of behaviour characteristic of it. According to Jung, the resulting predictable behavioural patterns form eight psychological types:

> + Extraverts with dominant sensing
> + Introverts with dominant sensing
> + Extraverts with dominant intuition
> + Introverts with dominant intuition
> + Extraverts with dominant thinking
> + Introverts with dominant thinking
> + Extraverts with dominant feeling
> + Introverts with dominant feeling

Myers and Briggs built on statements by Jung about the way in which the four mental processes interact, by adding a fourth dichotomy to the model, Judging/Perceiving, which describes how we manage the outer world – with either a judging or perceiving process. The introduction of this dichotomy enabled them

---

*The*
# MBTI PREFERENCES

---

**How are you energised?**

*Extraversion* ○————————————○ *Introversion*

**How do you prefer
to take in information?**

*Sensing* ○————————————○ *Intuition*

**How do you make decisions?**

*Thinking* ○————————————○ *Feeling*

**How do you deal
with the outer world?**

*Judging* ○————————————○ *Perceiving*

---

to incorporate an auxiliary function which supports and complements the dominant function in every type. Thus, Jung's model was refined to describe sixteen personality types.

So, according to the current theory, everyone has a preference for one of the two opposites on each of the four dichotomies. (We use both poles at different times but not at the same time and not with equal confidence.) The MBTI instrument reports a responder's preferences on the four dichotomies. The combined results then indicate a person's probable type – an underlying personality pattern resulting from the dynamic interaction of their four preferences, represented by a combination of four letters of the alphabet.

## *The*
# MBTI TYPES

| Dominant Function | Auxiliary Function | MBTI Type |
|---|---|---|
| Introverted Sensing | with Extraverted Thinking | ISTJ |
| Introverted Sensing | with Extraverted Feeling | ISFJ |
| Extraverted Sensing | with Introverted Thinking | ESTP |
| Extraverted Sensing | with Introverted Feeling | ESFP |
| Introverted Intuition | with Extraverted Thinking | INTJ |
| Introverted Intuition | with Extraverted Feeling | INFJ |
| Extraverted Intuition | with Introverted Thinking | ENTP |
| Extraverted Intuition | with Introverted Feeling | ENFP |
| Introverted Thinking | with Extraverted Sensing | ISTP |
| Introverted Thinking | with Extraverted Intuition | INTP |
| Extraverted Thinking | with Introverted Sensing | ESTJ |
| Extraverted Thinking | with Introverted Intuition | ENTJ |
| Introverted Feeling | with Extraverted Sensing | ISFP |
| Introverted Feeling | with Extraverted Intuition | INFP |
| Extraverted Feeling | with Introverted Sensing | ESFJ |
| Extraverted Feeling | with Introverted Intuition | ENFJ |

The supporting literature also provides rich descriptions of the sixteen types in terms of characteristic behaviour.

Critics of type approaches argue that individual differences cannot be captured adequately by placing people in one or other of a few all-or-none categories. Jung, himself, recognised this:

"One can never give a description of a type, no matter how complete, that would apply to more than one individual, despite the fact that in some ways it aptly characterises thousands of others. Conformity is one side of a man, uniqueness is the other."[19]

Acknowledging the criticism, the Jungian analyst and psychologist, Anthony Stevens, explains how Jungian typology can be helpful:

"On the whole, Jung's typology is best used in the way that one would use a compass: all typological possibilities are theoretically available to the Self, but it is useful to be able to establish those co-ordinates that one is using to chart one's course through life. Jung accepted that this course is never intractably fixed; it may at any time be subject to alteration. Viewed in this light, awareness of one's psychological type is not a constraint but a liberation, for it can open up new navigational possibilities in life, the existence of which one might otherwise never have discovered."[20]

It is not surprising, therefore, that the MBTI instrument should be so popular in organisations today. It has been translated into more than thirty languages, and more than 3.5 million questionnaires are distributed annually world-wide.

### II. c. A third lens on personality: Values.[21]

s noted above, the two most commonly referenced approaches to understanding personality today are trait and type approaches. Readers may, however, be interested in a third possibility for exploring patterns of behaviour – a values approach – provided by Milton Rokeach, the leading theorist in the field of values research.

Rokeach defines values as "socially shared conceptions of the desirable".[22] They are the learned resultants of external forces (e.g. societal goals and demands) and internal forces (i.e. individual needs) acting upon a person and, whether they are explicit and fully conceptualised, or implicit and unreflective, they serve as criteria to guide behaviour. From his extensive, cross-cultural studies, Rokeach was able to identify a relatively short list of thirty-six universal human values that he then organised into two categories: 'terminal' values and 'instrumental' values. Terminal values refer to beliefs or conceptions about ultimate goals or desirable end-states of existence which are worth striving for (such as 'happiness' or 'wisdom'); instrumental values refer to beliefs or conceptions about desirable modes of behaviour which are instrumental to the attainment of desirable end-states (such as behaving 'honestly' or 'responsibly').[23]

Using the mechanism of his 'Rokeach Value Survey' (1967), which invites responders to arrange the eighteen terminal values and the eighteen instrumental values in order of importance to them as guiding principles in their life,[24] Rokeach arrived at a conception of humans differing from one another not so much in terms of whether they possess particular terminal or instrumental values, but in the way they organise them to form value hierarchies or priorities.[25]

As the scholars, Keith Sanders and Erwin Atwood, explain, the prime assertion of the theory out of which the original Rokeach experiments were drawn is that, when we become aware, through self-confrontation, of contradictions between our conceptions of Self and our values, attitudes or behaviour, we will reorganise our values and attitudes and, thus, our behaviour to make them more consistent with our conceptions of Self.† The theory is based on the assumption that individuals hold a hierarchically ordered, interconnected belief system in which the most central elements are the conceptions or cognitions that they have of themselves. The 'master function' of the entire belief

† ON VALUES, ATTITUDES AND BEHAVIOUR *"Values may be thought of as global beliefs about desirable end-states underlying attitudinal and behavioural processes. Attitudes are seen to constitute cognitive and affective orientations toward specific objects or situations. Behavior generally is viewed as a manifestation of values and attitudes."*[26]

| TERMINAL VALUES | INSTRUMENTAL VALUES |
| --- | --- |
| A comfortable life | Ambitious |
| An exciting life | Broadminded |
| A sense of accomplishment | Capable |
| A world at peace | Cheerful |
| A world of beauty | Clean |
| Equality | Courageous |
| Family security | Forgiving |
| Freedom | Helpful |
| Happiness | Honest |
| Inner harmony | Imaginative |
| Mature love | Independent |
| National security | Intellectual |
| Pleasure | Logical |
| Salvation | Loving |
| Self-respect | Obedient |
| Social recognition | Polite |
| True friendship | Responsible |
| Wisdom | Self-controlled |

system is to maintain and, when possible, to enhance one's total conception of one's Self.[27] Rokeach's theory hence provides for a dynamic perspective of personality and, through his research, he was able to demonstrate that our values are, indeed, capable of undergoing enduring change (an experience which may be triggered, for example, by societal shifts or significant life events) with important consequences in terms of attitudinal and behavioural change.

The sociologist, Robin Williams, then investigated the causal relationship of values, recognising that neither conceptual clarity nor individual commitment are sufficient to guarantee particular behavioural outcomes. He concluded that it is only when values are 'activated' that they can influence conduct. In general terms, if personally consequential rewards are expected to result, the rate of conforming responses will be high; if punishments or deprivations are expected to result, the rate will be reduced.[28] He does recognise, of course, that under some conditions, people do express their strongly internalised values – i.e. they 'follow the dictates of conscience' – even when they know their behaviour will not be rewarded or, indeed, will be costly to them. He also notes that the causal link between values and behaviour is likely to become tighter with age, in part because increasing age affords the opportunity to develop more expansive and sophisticated levels of moral understanding, and in part because maturity is associated with a greater integration of internalised values with patterns of motivation (see the Moral stream).

Our values do, therefore, serve as criteria to guide our behaviour particularly, it seems, as we mature, and so Rokeach's work represents another lens through which personality may be viewed.

### III. How do we make sense of all this?

iven all the richness and complexity (and potential confusion) provided by these different approaches to understanding this important phenomenon of personality, I invited my professional storyteller colleague, Sue Hollingsworth, to write three stories to illustrate how it may influence the conduct of individuals in their day-to-day organisational lives. Welcome to your local zoo!

### III. a. Meet Nicola Moore, 34.

icola glanced at herself in the mirror. Her navy suit and peach blouse were perfect for the cameras. She hoped it would send the right message to her new staff as well: professional, competent, here to make a difference. She put a pinch of food into her fish tank, picked up her briefcase containing her notes for the television interview she had arranged for that afternoon, and slammed the door of her apartment on her way out.

As she climbed into her one-year-old Mercedes, she felt a glow of satisfaction. Who would have thought that she, Nicola Moore, from the largest council estate in the area, would ever have been able to afford this kind of car, or even a two-bedroom apartment right in the heart of the city? Yet again she sent up a quick prayer of gratitude to her parents whose drive and sacrifices had made it possible for her to go to university, the first one in her family to do so. She remembered the day she had told them that she wanted to study zoo and public facilities management.

"Will you get a pension with that sort of work, love?" asked her father.

"Probably, Dad. Depends on where I end up. I just know I want to make something of myself."

Her mother had not said anything but had beamed with pride, just as she had done last month when Nicola visited them to tell them that she had accepted the job of director at their local zoo.

"It won't be too much for you darling, will it? I read about those animal protesters in the paper last week. And they said that all the funding is going to be cut."

"Don't worry Mum. I'm used to all that. Look at how much money I've had to save as operations manager at the place I'm at now. I've got some good ideas for how to cut costs in this new role, and since I've been on that Advanced Media Skills training, I'm going to use the TV to help me get my point across."

"You're never going to be on the TV! I won't be able to live it down at the pub," her father chipped in.

"Free drinks, Dad, just think of the free drinks."

Nicola swung the car into the approach to the zoo. Her first day: her big chance to make a name for herself, not just in her home city but also in the field of zoo management. One or two protesters were arriving at the gates but they were not being disruptive. She parked, climbed out of her car, picked up her case, squared her shoulders and pushed open the main door of the office building.

"Good morning, Miss Moore." It was her personal assistant.

"Good morning, Caroline. Bring the diary into my office and let's get started."

Twenty minutes later, Nicola was satisfied that she would make an impact on her first day. She had already called a staff meeting for nine o'clock and, after a quick cup of coffee, walked briskly to the conference room.

There was a low buzz of conversation from the assembled thirty or so employees as she entered. Nicola knew they were worried about their jobs.

"Thank you all for coming. I realise you must be concerned about how things will change with my appointment. I want you to know that the survival of the zoo is my top priority and, as such, I will not flinch from making the tough decisions that need to be made. In order to secure our grants from the city council, we need to demonstrate that we are spending money in the most cost-effective way. To that end, I will be instituting a complete expenditure review beginning next week. We also need to attract other sources of revenue so that we are not so dependent on those grants. I will be putting together a small team to help target new sources of finance, especially from neighbouring businesses. Publicity from the protesters outside the gates has not been helpful. This afternoon I will be conducting the first of a series of media interviews with our local TV channel to put our point across to the public, and I plan to set up meetings with the community to enlist their support, too."

Nicola looked up from her notes. They were all still listening, which was good. "Are there any immediate questions?" she asked. A hand in the back row shot up.

"What about the animals, Miss Moore?"

"Good question. I plan to make the animals themselves the centrepiece of this media campaign. I want to encourage more people to come to the zoo and to understand the role that zoos play with regards to our social and cultural heritage. And, for that, we need to give the animals 'pride of place'. I will be looking at an 'adoption' scheme for local businesses which will focus on the most appealing and heart-warming of our residents. It is possible that, in the future, we may have to let go of some of our animals in order to facilitate this increased revenue but we will still maintain the high standards of care that this zoo is known for."

Nicola heard some mutterings from the people gathered. "Without these changes, it is likely that the zoo will face closure in the next five years, with a very uncertain future for both us and our animals. It's my job to make sure that doesn't happen. I look forward to working with you to ensure the zoo's survival."

After the meeting with the staff, Nicola had a meeting with the city council: men in suits whom she could talk to easily. Some of them found it hard to talk to her, though. Perhaps they were not used to dealing with women in senior positions? But others, she could see, were willing to listen to her and give her a chance.

The highlight of the day was the television interview. Nicola knew she 'looked the part' and felt confident in front of the cameras. She realised how effective every minute of air time could be. The presenter was a young man, even younger than she.

"I'm here outside our local zoo with new director, Nicola Moore. Nicola, could you tell us what you think the future of the zoo is?"

Nicola took a deep breath. "The zoo has been through hard times, Simon, and it is still facing some tough challenges. I took on this job because I believe in the service the zoo provides for the community, and I also believe local people want their zoo to continue. We have excellent staff, a wonderful record of working with nearby schools, and our animals are cared for to the highest standard."

"And what message do you have for the protesters who have been outside the gates for the past month now?"

Nicola turned to face the camera directly, as if she were speaking to the protesters themselves. "Everyone here cares for our animals. They cannot be released back to the wild. If our zoo closes, the animals will only suffer additional stress being moved around the world to other zoos. If you have the welfare of our animals at heart, please help us to help them. We will be setting up an animal sponsorship scheme shortly, and we *always* need more volunteers. Please get in contact with me personally at the zoo. I would be delighted to involve you."

The presenter moved smoothly to close the interview. "That was Nicola Moore with a direct appeal to the protesters here this evening. We'll be following the story of the zoo very closely in the next weeks, but now back to the studio."

When Nicola returned home that evening she felt satisfied. Her finance team were drawing up a detailed picture of expenditure and income for her; all the staff knew who she was; and she had had three minutes of air time on the evening news.

By the end of the week, she had produced a basic questionnaire to be completed by visitors to the zoo to investigate what, in particular, had attracted them. Nicola had been amazed to discover that this kind of information had not been collected in the past. She wanted to know if some animals pulled in more visitors than others, and whether she should spend precious funds refurbishing the café and restaurant which looked, at first glance, to be underperforming. She called a regular Monday morning meeting at 9.30 a.m. for all staff so that she could keep them informed about what was happening before they read or heard about it in the media, and she made a point of having something newsworthy for the press at least every two weeks.

When the responses on the questionnaires had been assessed, it was obvious there would have to be changes. The results showed that the majority of visitors were over fifty-five, coming with their grandchildren who were typically below school age. Most of the children wanted to see the lions and the seals. Nicola was quick to seize the opportunity provided by this, and wrote articles on the lions and seals for the local papers with lots of eye-catching photographs of the animals. She employed a marketing expert who devised a whole series of ways in which they could increase the number of people visiting the zoo, together with a 'Friends' scheme and some very attractive packages for schools which fitted with the required learning objectives of the national curriculum.

In her first year, visitor numbers improved by eight per cent and she was able to fend off the development sharks by showing the city council a well-thought-out plan for improving the facilities with the increased revenue expected in her second year. She had been interviewed on television seven times in that period, and had been featured in the local newspapers in seventy-four articles. At the end of her second year in office, she had masterminded the building of an entirely new enclosure for the lions which had been endorsed by a leading animal expert, and she had received the backing of the scientific community for a research project into the breeding habits of a rare monitor lizard. By the end of her third year, Nicola was recognised in the street by people who were used to seeing her as the 'face' of the zoo; the city council were not talking about 'development' any more; and the staff at the zoo had been increased by three to manage the additional work load.

"See, Mum," she said, "I knew I could do it, and I've really made a difference here. I'm even getting offers from national TV channels to present wildlife programmes."

"You're never going to do that, are you?" her mother gasped.

"Well, I'm thinking about it...."

### III. b. Now meet Philip Smythe, 67.

hil glanced at the headlines of the local paper open on the polished mahogany table, and then called up to his wife.

"I'm off now, darling. What are you doing today?"

"Having lunch with Gemma and the grandkids," came the answer as his wife appeared at the head of the stairs, still in her silk dressing gown. "I hope your first day goes well, Phil. Remember, it's a jungle out there!"

Phil laughed at the old joke which dated back to his glory days as director in a large city zoo in the north, and closed the front door behind him. He sniffed the morning air. The garden was looking wonderful. He and his wife had a new gardener who had made a lot of progress with the herbaceous borders. It was strange to be going back to work after nearly five years of 'retirement' but he was relishing it. He had always loved working in zoos – well, it was actually the animals he loved. He had grown up in Kenya on a farm up-country, where he had been used to being surrounded by animals. When he had had to attend boarding school in England at eight years old, he had been so lonely until he was taken to the zoo by a friend of the family, and was able to reconnect with animals again. He smiled, remembering how the zoo looked in those days, nearly sixty years ago, and now he was going back, back to that very same zoo again. But this time he was going to rescue it for future generations of children. Even though he had appeared to be very relaxed about the job offer to his friends on the city council, he believed passionately that all children should have the chance to make friends with animals, to understand their responsibility towards them, and he took his three grandchildren to the zoo whenever he could.

As he drove up to the zoo, he could see some of the protestors outside the gates. He stopped the car, climbed out, and wandered over to where they were sorting out banners and pouring cups of coffee from thermos flasks.

"Hello," he said, "I saw you lot on the news the other night, and you've made the front page in the local paper again today."

A young man and an older woman turned towards him, the woman speaking eagerly.

"Yes, it's wonderful that we were able to let people know what's going on here. I'm sure we'll get the zoo closed down in the end."

"What will happen to the animals?" asked Phil.

"Depends," said the young man. "Some of them could be released back into the wild, I suppose."

"But would they be able to fend for themselves? What happens if they can't make it?"

The woman spoke again. "It will save more animals being captured and put into such cruel places in the future and that's the most important thing."

Phil smiled. "I used to come here as a kid," he said. "I loved the zoo. I remember one day spending hours talking to the lions in the pit which used to be over by the back wall. I was convinced they understood every word I said. I bring my grandchildren here now and they love the animals, too. Where will children go to learn how to love animals if they can't come here?"

The woman smiled at his story. "I used to come here, too, when I was small but I've grown up now and I think we need to show our love for the animals by closing the place down."

"Thanks for the chat," said Phil, "maybe I'll see you later." Getting back into his car, he drove into the car park. He had a thoughtful expression on his face as he entered the office building. "Morning, Caroline. Good to see you again."

"Good morning, Mr Smythe, welcome to the zoo."

"Do please call me Phil. I must admit I never thought that one day I'd be walking into this building as director. It doesn't seem two minutes ago that I was eight years old with my nose pressed up against the giant reptile cage!"

"Well, they're still there, Phil. Perhaps you'd like to see them later?"

They exchanged a quick grin and then Phil said, "Actually, I think I'll make that my first stop this morning. It's a wonderful day for wandering around and meeting some of the staff. Is there anything scheduled for me that I should know about?"

Caroline consulted the diary on her computer screen. "Only a meeting with the city council at three."

"Right then, see you later."

Phil headed back through the door again. He spent several hours speaking with all the staff he encountered. He noticed how enthusiastic they were about their work. He saw how concerned they were about the animals. He could hear that they believed in the zoo, and when he told them stories about his visits with his grandchildren, they laughed and told him stories of their own. He ate lunch in the staff canteen, talked to the women in the catering unit, introduced himself to the last few staff members whom he had not met earlier, and then drove across the city to the council meeting.

"Hi, Phil, good to see you."

The chair of the council was an old friend. They had first met some thirty years ago at a conference and then, when Phil had retired and moved back to the city where he had enjoyed holidays as a child, their paths had crossed again at the golf club.

"Bob," he said, shaking hands. "Thanks for organising this meeting. It's good of you to get everyone together."

By now all the seats were filled and, after Bob had introduced him, the councillors asked him for his first impressions of the zoo.

"Very good," he said. "Committed staff, healthy animals, buildings are run down of course and the protesters outside the gate don't do us much good, but I'm sure I can handle them. Main problem is the developers putting pressure on you guys as far as I can see. Do you mind telling me the story?"

"The usual one, Phil," said Bob. "The zoo's a prime piece of real estate, smack in the centre of the city, and the developers know that the place is in trouble. We commissioned surveys from several large companies and I'll not hide the fact from you that the money we would make by selling the land would do the city an enormous amount of good."

Phil looked at each of the councillors in turn. "I know this is pushy," he said, "but you've asked me to turn the zoo around, and I've taken the job because I believe I can. However, I need to win people's confidence and inspire them to carry on. To do that, I'll need your assurance that you won't sell the zoo for three years. If I can't turn it around in that time, it won't be achievable, but I'll never do it at all if everyone thinks it's going to be sold from under our feet."

"And then what did they say, Phil?" Phil and his wife had eaten dinner, and his wife was curled up on the settee as he recounted his day to her.

"They agreed that I could have the three years! I asked them if I could go to the press with an announcement, and they said they would put it in writing to me by the end of the week. Darling, I really feel like I'm going to make a difference there. Now there's hope for these animals and all the people there, too." His wife smiled at him, fondly.

"And you'll be able to recreate the zoo of your childhood, won't you?" she teased.

"Well, yes, there is that, too...."

The rest of the week, Phil walked and talked his way through the zoo. It was only on Thursday that the protesters, whom he had spoken to each morning since his arrival, realised who he was. By then, they had heard his stories about growing up in Kenya, surrounded by animals; they knew how important the zoo had been to him as a lonely child at boarding school; they had seen photos of his grandchildren smiling outside the monkey house. They knew he cared. So when he stopped at the gates that morning and told them who he was, that he was going to announce a

three-year 'period of hope' to the press on Monday morning, and
that he was also inviting them to participate with him in a joint
press conference, they listened. He led them into his office for
coffee, talked to them about his ideas for the zoo, and asked them
how they thought it could be improved. Within a very short space
of time the protesters were volunteering to run a community out-
reach programme. Then, on Monday morning, letter from the
city council in his hand, Phil faced the cameras outside the zoo
with a delegation of the former protesters. He announced the
breathing space of three years, and the protesters declared their
willingness to join together with other groups supporting the zoo
to develop a new way forward. The headline in the local paper
that evening read 'New Boss Brings Zoo Hope'.

That was not the end of the story, of course; it was only the
beginning. Over the following weeks, Phil created a tightly knit
top team to whom he delegated vigorously, so that he was free to
continue to tell his stories of the past, present and future zoo. His
vast experience made him a good judge of people; and, because he
knew he did not want to stay in the job forever, he started the process of training Sandra to be his replacement. She was a woman
with an impressive academic background who had worked at the
zoo since leaving university eleven years ago; and, within a year,
she became his deputy. Staff morale improved enormously as Phil
made sure he wandered around regularly, talking informally to
everyone whilst also getting to know the animals. And as for his
grandchildren, they thought he was 'the tops' when the keeper
took them with him to see the elephants!

When his three years in the post came to an end, he attended
a meeting of the city council with Sandra, at which it was decided
that the zoo should stay open as attendance figures were rising
rapidly. Phil agreed to remain for one more year on the condition
that he would be replaced by Sandra, who would, by then, have
had enough experience to assume the role of director.

As Phil himself said as he handed over to Sandra, four years after taking up the position, "It's been a fantastic opportunity to restore our zoo to its rightful place at the centre of our local community. Now that we're on an even keel, financially, and with visitor numbers rising, the future holds all sorts of exciting prospects."

"Yes," said Sandra, "and I'd like to tell you about the plans we have to raise funds for a brand new reptile house with all the latest technology, so that the next generation of children will also be able to press their noses to the glass in wonder, just like you did when you were a little boy."

Everyone roared and clapped with approval, and Phil blushed as he took a bow, before turning again to Sandra to hear more about this great idea.

### III. c. Finally, meet David Morgan, 45.

uick, catch that chicken!" David dropped the small, black rucksack he used instead of a briefcase, and dived on top of the chicken which was making its escape through the kitchen.

"That was funny, Daddy, wasn't it?" beamed his daughter, looking angelic in her school uniform as feathers scattered in all directions and the new puppy wriggled in her arms.

"Thanks darling," said his wife as she clomped wearily up the muddy path in her Wellington boots.

"Any eggs?" he asked.

She took the chicken from him. "Only two."

David's teenage son from his first marriage, Tom, drifted in, munching on toast and plugged into his iPod just as he seemed to be perpetually these days.

"Hey, Dad, you're gonna be late." He grinned. It was not often that he had the opportunity to say that line to his father. Usually it was the other way around.

"Damn!" David grabbed his rucksack and his waterproof jacket from the hook on the back of the door, kissed his wife, ruffled the hair of his son and daughter, and ran out of the house, tripping over the cat that had taken to ambushing anyone who was trying to leave in a hurry.

Moments later he was weaving through the morning traffic on his bicycle. The zoo was about twenty-five minutes away, and at last he had time to think. His head was buzzing with ideas about how to attract more educational trips to the school, and how the local action group could become more involved – perhaps he could invite them to form a practical task force to help with the dilapidated areas of the grounds? And as for the protesters, he had some ideas there, too!

David sped into the entrance of the zoo and looked for a place to park his bike. But there *was* no area for bikes. He made a mental note to sort that out. He wanted the zoo to be supporting environmentally sound principles throughout its operations. Thinking about it, perhaps they should offer a discount on the entry price to people who arrived on foot or on a bike. That should be newsworthy and ethically sound. And why wasn't there a bus stop right outside the front gate? He would have to tackle that, too. Taking off his helmet and clips, he paused outside the main door of the office block. How he had longed for this day! At last he was a director and not a deputy director, able to stand or fall on his own merits. He had been working towards this position for so many years, since taking his first job at an inner city farm when he was a teenager. That was when he had realised that he wanted to work with animals. His parents found it very strange as they had not even had pets when he was a child. David smiled, thinking of the menagerie which lived in his house now, and how his daughter, Beatrice, loved them.

He pushed the door open. His personal assistant, Caroline, was waiting for him at her desk.

"Good morning, Mr Morgan. Welcome to the zoo."

David shook her hand. "Good morning, Caroline. I'm looking forward to working with you. Could you bring the diary and a mug of tea through to me and we'll get started?"

After an hour, Caroline ran off with a long list of things to do. David, meanwhile, wanted to enlist his marketing assistant, John Simmonds, in his plan to approach the education authority. He knew he would need financial assistance from them to launch what he privately called his 'Education Offensive'. He had already prepared an outline of a proposal to provide detailed support to biology, geography and art teachers in local schools; now he needed John to convert his ideas into a presentation pack. He invited him to join him in his office, and was really pleased to discover that he was a very competent young man who took up the challenge without blinking an eye.

David also wanted to make contact with the leaders of the 'Save Our Zoo' support group in the community. They seemed to be particularly well organised and he thought that he should try to meet with them straightaway. At that moment, the telephone rang.

"I've got Mrs Cousins for you, Mr Morgan," said Caroline. She transferred the call and David immediately engaged with the likeable woman on the end of the line who turned out to be the mainstay of the 'Save Our Zoo' movement.

"Mrs Cousins, thank you for contacting me. I wonder whether we could meet this afternoon, as I'd like to involve your group in the future development of the zoo."

"Of course, Mr Morgan. You probably know already that we have an informal membership of about eighty people and we're all very committed to the future of the zoo."

David was curious about this as he had no idea why people had joined the group. "What kind of people are they? And why are they giving their time?" he asked.

"They're mostly professional people like myself – I'm a lawyer but an 'at-home mother' with three children at the moment. I head up the group because all my kids love the place. We have teachers, the local librarian, the Methodist minister's wife, two doctors, a rather well-known actor who lives close by who's willing to lend his name, a researcher, a fireman, a couple of social workers...."

"Whoa, stop! That's an incredible resource for us. If you'd like to bring two of your colleagues in as well, if they're free, I'd be very grateful."

"I'll see what I can do. Shall we say 2.30 p.m.?"

David felt very positive after the call and even more so when John Simmonds came back to him with some useful suggestions for how to tailor his ideas for the education authority. He had researched the national curriculum and quickly spotted some opportunities to tie school visits much more closely to the key requirements of the curriculum. David reviewed his ideas thoughtfully and then telephoned his wife.

"Darling, it's me."

"How's it going so far? How do they all seem?"

"It's going well and my marketing guy, John, is making an excellent start on those ideas for developing school visits that I told you about. It suddenly occurred to me, though, that Beatrice might be able to help. I know she's only six but how do you feel about her coming to the zoo with me one day? I could invite the press in to take some photos of us and maybe have a few words with her? She really loves the zoo."

There was silence at the end of the line and David could almost hear his wife's brain processing his question.

"I think we should talk to her this evening when you come home. If she's not shy then I can see it would be helpful. But David," she paused for a moment, "not if she doesn't want to."

"Thanks, darling, that's great. I'll see you later."

Sally Cousins was a marvel. She arrived at 2.30 p.m. sharp with the actor and the local librarian in tow, and did not waste a minute.

"Look Mr Morgan, we don't want to just sit on the sidelines here. We're willing to put our time and energy into helping the zoo. Considering our membership, we wondered if you would be interested in us becoming a task force of some description. Is there anything you need help with?"

David leaned back with a sigh of relief as another piece of the jigsaw fitted into place. He looked at the three of them.

"Yes," he said, "there is, actually. Would some of your team be willing to go into schools, libraries, youth clubs, wherever young people and children meet, and help present some stories and ideas about the zoo to them? John Simmonds is putting together a whole load of information for me and it seems to me that you, Keith," he turned to the actor, "would be ideally placed to help train people to give inspiring presentations." There followed a lively conversation and by 4.00 p.m. the main details of an activity plan were in place.

By the end of his first week, arrangements had been made for a dedicated zoo bus, painted in black and white zebra stripes, to stop right outside the zoo gates. A designated bicycle parking zone had been established. A prototype of the education pack had been designed as a result of the media photo opportunity with John, David and Beatrice (who had been only too happy to have an extra visit to the zoo with Daddy). Support had also come from a very unexpected angle: his son, Tom.

"Hey, Dad, I don't mind doing my bit, too, you know. Why don't I come over with some of my mates and help on a Saturday morning with something? I'm fed up with how the local paper is always running down young people. We're not afraid of hard work and it'll be a laugh."

And that was how the Saturday morning Zoo Club started. David arranged for Tom and seven of his friends to do some gardening that first weekend. He provided lunch for them, the press turned up, and a lot of good work was done. The next Saturday there were a dozen of them and, before long, thirty or more young people were arriving every Saturday morning to volunteer for all kinds of jobs. They became very friendly with the protesters outside the zoo gates who were mostly young people, too, and, after a while, one or two of the protesters actually joined in to discover what was going on inside the gates – what it was that all these other young people were so enjoying.

And that was the beginning of the end of the protests. David's greatest achievement, however, was with the education authority. He obtained permission to launch a whole campaign of targeted projects for specific subjects which linked with the national curriculum and, within six months, the number of school visits had quadrupled. Added to that was the interest the 'Save Our Zoo' group generated at the libraries and in other clubs and groups; and, after a year, the zoo reported the biggest increase in visitors under the age of eighteen in the whole country. David became a recognised authority on how to involve the local community in supporting zoos, and often hosted conferences on community involvement during the week on the zoo premises.

After three years, with visitor numbers soaring, and with the 'Save Our Zoo' group renaming itself the 'Support Our Zoo' group, there was a waiting list for the Saturday morning Zoo Club. David published a book on his experiences of involving the local community. With some wonderful animal photography, warm and witty text, and inspiring stories from the volunteers, it sold more copies than David had ever hoped it would. The inscription on the inside front cover read, "To my family, my most important community, without whom none of this would have happened."

### III. d. Questions for reflection.

ow you have read these three stories, I invite you to respond to the following questions which have been formulated to explore the relationship between the personalities of our three characters and their behaviour:

1. If you were asked to describe in a sentence or two the personalities of each of the three protagonists, how would you do that?

2. Which of the thirty facets from the Five Factor Model do you recognise in each of the characters?

3. Which characters provide a realistic and practical perspective ('sensing' types in the MBTI typology) and which provide connections and meanings ('intuitive' types)? Which characters focus on tasks ('thinking' types), and which focus on people's interactions ('feeling' types)?

4. Which of the terminal and instrumental values would you identify as the guiding principles of the characters' lives?

5. If you were a candidate for the deputy directorship of the zoo, which one of these three personalities would you prefer to work with and why?

6. Should you face the same circumstances as these characters, which aspects of your personality (traits, type elements and values) would be apparent?

### *IV. Conclusion.*

ersonality – what it is, what determines it, how it drives behaviour, how much it is influenced by situational factors, and how stable it is – has been a subject of fascination since earliest times, and there is much disagreement still amongst the theorists on all these matters. There is general agreement, however, that it *is* personality which causes our behaviour to be (relatively) consistent, and which also causes each of us to behave differently from each other. Frameworks aplenty have been developed to provide us with a lens through which we can view our own personality, and those who have used them report that they are helpful: they illuminate aspects of who we are and explain why we may behave in certain ways in certain circumstances. With this aware-

ness we also discover that we have choices – to behave, in a given situation, in accordance with our personality traits, our personality type and our current hierarchy of values, or to select our response from the broader span of possibilities that we now realise exists. Making such choices consciously enables us, of course, to be more effective in a wider and wider range of scenarios whilst still being authentic. I encourage readers, therefore, to experiment with one or more of these frameworks. Equipped, then, with an understanding of the human development road (from Chapter One), of the challenges which may lie ahead (from Chapter Two), and with some knowledge of who we are, we will be ready to find a Guide for the journey – the subject of the next chapter. But, before we move on, we can summarise this chapter with some additions to our list of rules of the road:

### *The rules of the road.*

1. The human development journey begins in infancy and, if growth continues, may extend into late adulthood and even until death (some, of course, may say that it extends beyond death).

2. The path that we, as travellers, follow is one of many distinct stages, each of which represents a clear, qualitative transformation of thinking and being.

3. The strengths of one stage ultimately become its limitations, a realisation which nudges us to the next stage of our growth.

4. We progress from one stage to the next by the agency of two fundamental capacities: transcendence and inclusion.

5. Research has consistently demonstrated that these stages cannot be bypassed without some compromise.

6. Each stage of the journey offers a new set of challenges (intellectual, social, moral, emotional, psychological and even spiritual challenges) which flow as streams of development through the basic stages of development.

7. These streams unfold as the stages unfold, by the same agencies of transcendence and inclusion, and also with their own dynamic.

8. If, in our determination to press onwards, we choose not to confront all the challenges available to us in the streams of development, we will arrive at the next stage of our development with some of our potential unrealised, with an imbalance in our sphere of total capability.

9. To function as a fully integrated Self, therefore, we must recognise our development gaps and then seek out those stream-specific learning experiences which will enable us to attend to them.

10. How we embrace these learning experiences will be influenced, in some measure, by our own personality.

11. The more we understand our personality, the more we understand the behavioural choices available to us.

12. Knowing when and how to act 'in character' and when and how to act 'out of character' – whilst still being authentic – equips us to be more effective in a wider and wider range of situations.

# FINDING
# MERLIN

# A MAGICIAN
## FOR A GUIDE

## · CHAPTER FOUR ·
# A Magician for a Guide

### *I. The archetype of the helper.*

arl Jung, in his extensive study of the myths and legends of many cultures, observes that the two most commonly formulated motifs to be found in them are the image of the Hero, and the image of his helper, the Wise Old Man.[1] Of the helper, Jung notes that although he may present in many different forms (as magician, doctor, priest, teacher, professor or grandfather, for example[2]), he always personifies knowledge, reflection, insight, wisdom, cleverness and intuition, and also moral qualities such as goodwill and readiness to help.[3] Jung notes, too, that the role of the helper is always pivotal to the successful conclusion of these ancient stories: it is "when the hero is in a hopeless and desperate situation from which only profound reflection or a lucky idea… can extricate him"[4] that he appears.

### *II. The helper of the Arthurian legend.*

he principal helper of the Arthuriad is, of course, the magician, Merlin, Counsellor to all the Dark Age Kings and Guide of the Grail quest. The son of a princess and an incubus (a spirit which lives between the earth and the moon, part human and part angel), he possesses more than ordinary powers. He can see beyond the world as it is apprehended by others, to glimpse truths otherwise hidden – the truth of the connectedness of all things, and the connectedness of this world with the transcendental realm. So it is that he can materialise in different guises and perform feats of great artistry; he can interpret the meaning of astrological events; he can see into the future; he can see into the past; and he can see into the hearts of men. Shape-shifter, confidant,

seer, sage, strategist, kingmaker but ultimately also a man, himself, whose fate is to be imprisoned forever by a beautiful seduc-
tress who persuades him to reveal the secrets of his mysterious
arts – this is the image of Merlin which has fascinated poets,
storytellers, dramatists and now screenwriters for more than 800
years. Without him, Vortigern would not have confronted his
own evil, Uther Pendragon would not have defeated the invading
Saxons, Arthur would not have been conceived nor crowned King,
and neither Perceval nor Galahad would have found the Grail.

### III. The tyranny of individualism.

he heroes of the stories of the past may have been
willing to accept the help of a guide but in today's
societies, and in Western societies in particular,
we are often reluctant to turn to others for assistance when we face challenging situations. Furthermore, as we noted in Chapter One, the working environments
where we spend most of our waking hours typically attach great
value to self-reliance and personal achievement, and so they *foster*
us in this over-investment in ourselves. And now, in the second
decade of the twenty-first century, there are new forces at play in
modern organisational systems which only reinforce the elevation
of the individual work ethic over the group work ethic. Traditional structures of hierarchical layers of supervision, decision-
making and control, are giving way rapidly to flatter, more
empowered and globally distributed arrangements in which
people operate at the hub of their own, individualised networks.
So if, and when, we do achieve seniority in these new, more disparate formations, we discover that leadership, which was ever a
lonely occupation, is now an even lonelier one.

In the meantime, of course, our personal development challenges will be manifesting themselves in the way we perform our
organisational (and life) roles. Perhaps, for example, we need
to become more tolerant of ambiguity so that we can embrace
those situations which occur regularly with positions of influence,

## Who was Merlin?

he character of Merlin seems to have been drawn, at least in part, from a figure who may have lived in earlier times. This 'original' Merlin was a sixth-century Briton. Crazed by a ferocious inter-British battle (recorded in the *Annales Cumbriae* under the year 573 CE) at Arthuret, located eight miles north of Carlisle, he wandered through the Caledonian Forest in southern Scotland, an inspired madman, gifted or cursed with second sight. His name was Lailoken, and his story is recorded in the twelfth-century *Life of St Kentigern* (the patron saint of Glasgow) by Joceline of Furness, and two related fifteenth-century narratives.

As the Saxon invaders overwhelmed the Scottish Lowlands, Britons fled south to Wales. They took with them their legendary heritage, and the tales of their northern heroes subsequently appeared in Welsh literature. The story of Lailoken and his soothsayings was among them. Scholars believe that it was crystallised in verse in the ninth century and written down between 850 and 1050. This early material has not survived but fragments do exist of six poetic monologues from the thirteenth century spoken by the prophet (here called Myrddin, a Welsh sobriquet for Lailoken). In these Welsh poems, he is a dignified figure, suffering deeply in exile, afraid of powerful enemies, lamenting a happier past, yet also uttering great public predictions which foreshadow a Celtic revival after the Britons' struggles against the Normans and the English.

As a literary figure, Merlin is the creation of Geoffrey of Monmouth, a Welsh cleric and chronicler of the twelfth century, who wrote three works (in Latin) which have come down to us: *The Prophecies of Merlin* (originally conceived as a separate volume), his great *History of the Kings of Britain* (which incorporates the *Prophecies*), and the less significant *Life of Merlin*. It is likely that he knew something of the legend of Myrddin when he was writing his *History* (the 'Wild Man of the Woods' is a popular theme in the folklore of many cultures). But his principal source for the character of Merlin is another legend, a clearly fictional story of a prophet boy, Ambrosius, found in the ninth-century *Historia Brittonum* (traditionally, but probably erroneously, attributed to the Welsh cleric and historian, Nennius). In this story, Ambrosius, born of a princess and an incubus, has special, supernatural powers which the usurper Vortigern, King of Britain, employs to explain why the foundations of his new fortified city are collapsing. Ambrosius predicts that if Vortigern's men dig beneath the foundations they will discover two serpents (or dragons), one of which will be white, and one red. The dig begins and the serpents are revealed, whereupon they wake, fight, and the red one drives the white one away.[5] Ambrosius then explains that the battle of the serpents foretells the defeat of the Saxons for the red one symbolises the Britons, and the white one, the invaders; and he advises Vortigern to build his citadel elsewhere.

In his *History*, Geoffrey of Monmouth renames the prescient boy 'Merlin'[6] and recasts him as a magician in the medieval tradition, as a counsellor to three of the Dark Age Kings (Vortigern, Aurelius and Uther Pendragon), and as the contriver of the conception of Arthur. Seventy years later, the French romancer, Robert de Boron, provides him with a greater purpose: he is the architect of Arthur's birth, early education, and ascent to the throne through the mechanism of the Sword in the Stone, and he oversees the construction of the Round Table. But now he is also the prophet of the Grail quest and guide to the Grail Knight, Perceval. And a century after this development, Merlin is recast once more in a prose continuation of Robert de Boron's story (in the *Vulgate Cycle*), as a man of flesh and blood who becomes infatuated with the beautiful but wily Niniane (Malory's Nenyve, Tennyson's Vivien), who beguiles him into teaching her his mysterious arts, and then imprisons him forever in a tower in the Forest of Broceliande. In Sir Thomas Malory's *Le Morte Darthur*, written a decade or two later, Merlin foretells his own fate – that he will die imprisoned by Nenyve, this time in a rock – but still he cannot resist her, a fall which prefigures the destruction of the whole fellowship of the Round Table (precipitated, of course, by Lancelot's adulterous love for Arthur's queen, Guenivere, and the hatred of the King's traitorous son, Mordred, who mortally wounds him in the last battle before he is slain, himself, at his father's own hand).[7]

*Magic: making meaning in a pre-scientific world.*

 eoffrey of Monmouth's representation of Merlin draws heavily on medieval ideas of the important practice of magic, a system of beliefs which has ancient origins. In every early human society, archaeological evidence (some of it 30,000 years old) suggests that an animistic (or magical) world-view emerged, which linked the people, the land and the cosmos. Magic was the medium of connection, offering an explanation of the cause-and-effect relationship between an act and its consequence, and its earliest technicians were shamans. Shamans were men or women who were often set apart from others by a distinctive sign (such as being born 'in the caul') or a deformity. They were, it was assumed, 'called' by the spirits. Using specialist techniques, they could enter a trance or an alternative state of consciousness, and thereby communicate with the spirit realms for information, advice or knowledge, in order to protect or heal their community.

European magicians of the Middle Ages were reputed to have special powers derived from their shamanic forbears – the capacity to change shape, to fly through the air, and to disappear without a trace. But, as contact with the Arab world was established in the mid-eleventh century, new ideas arrived from the East, and magicians acquired additional skills. They had always been diviners (using techniques such as palm reading) but, with new notions of the astrological pattern of the universe, they could now link the celestial and the earthly realms, and so predict not only an individual's future, but larger social and political events, too, by studying comets, eclipses and the movement of the planets. Magic was not just the preserve of common people. It also informed the understanding of Kings and Queens, who employed personal astrologers and gave great credence to their advice.

From the East also came the most mysterious (and later forbidden) art of alchemy. Despite the chicanery and pretentiousness which surrounded this magical practice (satirised so adroitly by Ben Jonson in his play, *The Alchemist*, of 1610), the motives of many of its practitioners were altruistic and laudable. By means of their alchemical experiments which were intended to deliver the elixir of life (a universal cure) and the philosopher's stone (a substance which would transmute base metals to gold), they sought to penetrate the secrets of the cosmos – of nature, life, death, eternity and infinity. Alchemy was also an esoteric technique with spiritual goals. Its practitioners believed that, through their work, they could transmute not just substances but also themselves – become perfect human beings.

The rational perspective of today's Western cultures (unlike the analogical perspective of the East, where shamans still practise) discounts a hidden dimension to our earthly experience. But, during the medieval period, when the Arthurian legend was evolving, magicians were venerated (and feared) by all: they could interpret the world, and direct the forces and powers inherent in the universe, in ways not comprehended by ordinary men. And Merlin, as he was originally conceived by Geoffrey of Monmouth, and as he is represented by subsequent writers of the period, is one such mage.[8] ✤

where no clear answers present and judgement is the measure of most things (see the Intellectual stream). Or perhaps we need to learn to manage our impatience and frustration with members of our team in order to create more trust (see the Emotional stream). Or perhaps we need to dedicate more time to introspective practices to enable us to exercise our leadership more consciously and more authentically (see the Psychological stream). These are real and important challenges that we are obliged to address for both ourselves and those we lead. Our working environment will, in all probability, offer opportunities aplenty to do so, but, if we are to take advantage of them, it is likely that we will require help from others who have experience of overcoming the difficulties we face.

How might we find this help? To begin with, we need to know where we are now – what progress we have already made on our journey of growth. We also need to know where we *could* be. Then we need to make the choice to move forward, in the full knowledge that the way ahead will not be easy. Only then will we be ready and able to identify the right guide – or guides – to help us in our endeavour.

### *IV. Where are you now? Where could you be?*

now thyself' was one of the wise pronouncements of Apollo, revealed to the Delphic oracle and carved into a lintel of the temple at Delphi. As we have recognised since the time of the ancients, therefore, knowledge of Self is essential if we are to master Self. So, in order to travel further along the human development road with all our potential available to us, we must consider our current position from two aspects:

1.  We must first understand which *stage* of development we have reached (see Chapter One). If we are working in an organisation, we have probably achieved the Organisational stage but have we achieved the World-Centric stage?

    • *Organisational stage*: My concern is to preserve my autonomy, and seek group recognition of it in my organisation.

• *World-Centric stage:* Now I can embrace a truly world
view, not just in word but in deed, too.

2.  Secondly, we must understand how far we have progressed
along the various *streams* of development, remembering that,
as each one unfolds with its own dynamic, our progress along
them is unlikely to be uniform (see Chapter Two).

Self-reflection, inviting feedback from others, and 'making sense'
of our reflections and feedback, are the means by which we discover where we are now and, by implication, where we could be.

My main purpose in writing this book is to enable readers,
most of whom, I assume, will have reached the Organisational
stage, to progress to the World-Centric stage, and to function
there as a fully integrated Self. To assist you in this endeavour, I
have formulated a set of questions for self-reflective inquiry. They
are intended to help you explore your
specific development gaps. (They do
not, incidentally, focus on what you *do*
in terms of the activities of your role
because, to live at the World-Centric
stage, of course, you must separate
yourself from your activities.) In the
course of my career, I have been privileged to work with many leaders in
many different contexts and cultures,
and so I have crafted these questions
to capture the challenges that I have
discovered people who make their organisation 'happen' typically face as they make the transition to, or become embedded in,
the World-Centric stage. I invite you to read through them and
decide which answer ('a' or 'b') describes you, on balance, most
accurately. Try to be as honest with yourself as you can – introspection should not necessarily be a self-affirming practice!

> *"Through a complex
> of factors, our conscious
> self-concept almost always
> diverges to a greater or lesser
> degree from the reality of the
> person we actually are. 'We'
> are almost always either less
> or more competent than we
> believe ourselves to be. The
> unconscious, however,
> knows who we really
> are." – PECK[9]*

So, to begin with, how big is your world? As an initial point of
reference, have you made the transition yet to the World-Centric
stage?

HALLMARKS OF THE
# WORLD-CENTRIC STAGE

| Hallmarks | Questions for self-reflection |
|---|---|
| *You have separated yourself from your activities.* | ❖ Do you define yourself, in the main, by:<br>  a. What you do in your organisational role? *or*<br>  b. As someone who uses your corporate role as a vehicle for Self-expression and connection with others?<br><br>❖ Do you want to be known for:<br>  a. What you do? *or* b. Who you are? |
| *You have released yourself from a socio-centric stance.* | ❖ Do you expend more energy:<br>  a. Defending your social or cultural group from the 'outside'? *or*<br>  b. 'Bringing the outside in'?<br><br>❖ What do you value more about yourself?<br>  a. The person you are now, as the product of your social and cultural experiences? *or*<br>  b. The person you could become by integrating new experiences from other social and cultural milieux into your sense of Self? |
| *You view the world as one territory, one space.* | ❖ Is your attention focused more upon:<br>  a. Events taking place locally or nationally? *or*<br>  b. Events taking place on the world stage?<br><br>❖ Do you consider yourself to be:<br>  a. A citizen of your country? *or*<br>  b. A member of the global community? |

Now ask yourself if you have work to do in the six streams of development in order to promote your attainment of the World-Centric stage if you have not already achieved it, or, if you have done so, to be able to function there with all the potential which will be available to you when you have overcome the many and various challenges associated with this stage.

---

WORKING IN THE

# INTELLECTUAL STREAM

| Challenges | Questions for self-reflection |
|---|---|
| *To see reality as compound and multi-faceted, to unite and integrate ideas, and to embrace ambiguity, uncertainty, and flux.* | ❖ Do you prefer to understand situations, events, opportunities, problems:<br>    a. In terms of their constituent parts?<br>    *or*<br>    b. In terms of their 'wholeness'?<br><br>❖ When faced with seemingly incompatible alternatives, do you look for:<br>    a. What divides them? *or*<br>    b. What resolves them?<br><br>❖ How do you respond to ambiguity, uncertainty, and flux?<br>    a. With frustration? *or*<br>    b. With curiosity? |
| *To participate in group thinking.* | ❖ When you encounter problems, do you:<br>    a. Rely on your own knowledge and intellect to find a solution? *or*<br>    b. Bring together a diverse group of people to explore their perspectives in order to find a solution? |

(continued on following page)

*To participate in group thinking (cont'd).*

❖ When you are faced with different or contradictory perspectives in a group, do you:

    a. Assume there is a right perspective – one with which the group just needs to agree or align itself? *or*

    b. Use the group to explore the different perspectives available and develop a new or unique insight which, previously, did not exist?

---

WORKING IN THE

# SOCIAL STREAM

| Challenge | Questions for self-reflection |
|---|---|
| *To relate to, adapt to, and function with, other people well.* | ❖ Do you form new relationships with others with the intention of:<br>  a. Being yourself? *or*<br>  b. Discovering who the other person is?<br><br>❖ How would you describe your relationship with your partner, friends and colleagues?<br>  a. Established, steady, fixed? *or*<br>  b. A dynamic sequence of interpersonal negotiations?<br><br>❖ Are the primary purposes of your relationships:<br>  a. Security, affiliation, achievement? *or*<br>  b. Developing perspective, collaboration, learning? |

### WORKING IN THE
# MORAL STREAM

| Challenges | Questions for self-reflection |
|---|---|
| *To recognise that your own reference group's definition of 'right' and 'wrong' is only one among many.* | ❖ Your reference group's definition of what is 'right' and what is 'wrong' is the 'correct' one:  a. True? *or* b. False?<br><br>❖ When your understanding of what is 'right' or what is 'wrong' is challenged by your real-world experience, do you:<br>  a. Reassert your moral position as the 'correct' one? *or*<br>  b. Revise your understanding to incorporate new insights? |
| *To make distinctions about which ethical principles are the most conducive to the development of humankind.* | ❖ Do you spend time reflecting upon the ethical standards which make for a good society?  a. No? *or* b. Yes?<br><br>❖ Are you prepared to challenge cultural standards which breach the human rights of those whom they affect (notwithstanding any expected opposition from those who would defend them)?<br>  a. No? *or* b. Yes? |
| *To formulate a set of self-chosen ethical principles and be willing to take action to defend them.* | ❖ Would you prefer to be guided by:<br>  a. A set of conventional moral rules defined by others for you? *or*<br>  b. A set of unconventional moral rules which you have chosen for yourself?<br><br>❖ Are you willing to take personal risk to disobey unjust laws?<br>  a. No? *or* b. Yes? |

# EMOTIONAL STREAM

| Challenges | Questions for self-reflection |
|---|---|
| To recognise the specific feelings that trigger-stimuli arouse in you. | ❖ How would you describe your emotional responses? a. Spontaneous? or b. Considered?<br><br>❖ In most circumstances, do you 'feel' your emotions before you express them? a. No? or b. Yes? |
| To understand those feelings – why the stimuli are emotionally arousing to you. | ❖ Do you experience emotions as:<br>   a. Feelings which result from external events? or<br>   b. Feelings which result from your internal interpretation of events?<br><br>❖ When you notice a pattern occurring in your emotional responses, do you reflect upon why you react in the way you do to the particular trigger-stimulus? a. No? or b. Yes? |
| To control maladaptive bodily responses. | ❖ Do you receive feedback which suggests that you could express your positive emotions more constructively? a. Yes? or b. No?<br><br>❖ Do you receive feedback which suggests that you could express your negative emotions more constructively? a. Yes? or b. No? |
| To select, consciously, appropriate responses to stimuli from a large and nuanced repertoire of possible reactions. | ❖ Do you experience emotion as a form of energy that you can channel consciously? a. No? or b. Yes?<br><br>❖ When you experience a trigger-situation, do you recognise it as such, and then select an appropriate emotional response from a range of possible options? a. No? or b. Yes? |

## WORKING IN THE
# PSYCHOLOGICAL STREAM

| *Challenges* | *Questions for self-reflection* |
|---|---|
| *To respect the individuality of Self and others.* | ❖ Can you tell 'the story of you' – who you are, why you are who you are, and even who you seek to be?<br>　　a. No? *or* b. Yes?<br>❖ Do you value others because they are:<br>　　a. Similar to you? *or*<br>　　b. Different from you? |
| *To construct interdependent relationships.* | ❖ Do your relationships matter to you for their own sake?　a. No? *or* b. Yes?<br>❖ How would you describe your relationships with those adults to whom you are 'close'?<br>　　a. Mutually supportive, warm and loving? *or*<br>　　b. Genuinely intimate (i.e. constructed to meet each others' identity needs in more-or-less equal measure)? |
| *To cope with inner conflict.* | ❖ Is inner conflict:<br>　　a. Avoidable? *or* b. Inevitable?<br>❖ When you experience inner conflict:<br>　　a. Do you externalise it (i.e. look to circumstances, events or other people to explain or solve it for you)? *or*<br>　　b. Do you muster the courage to deal with it yourself? |

*(continued on following page)*

## WORKING IN THE
# PSYCHOLOGICAL STREAM
### (cont'd)

| Challenges | Questions for self-reflection |
|---|---|
| *To be interested in self-development and more concerned with self-fulfilment than achievement.* | ❖ Do you invest as much (in terms of time, effort and resources) in your personal development as you do in your professional development?<br>    a. No? *or* b. Yes?<br><br>❖ Do you reflect periodically upon the question, 'What is my life's work?'<br>    a. No? *or* b. Yes? |
| *To achieve a consolidated sense of identity, i.e. 'self-actualisation'.* | ❖ Abraham Maslow believed that 'self-actualisation' is only available to us when we have achieved autonomy; experienced an enduring, loyal, post-romantic love relationship; found our calling; developed our own system of values; shed perfectionistic illusions and become realistic; made our peace with death; learned how to be patient and compassionate; become post-ambivalent about parents and elders, power and authority; become knowledgeable and educated enough to open the possibility of becoming wise; and mustered the courage to be unpopular, to be unashamed about being openly virtuous etc. Have you met all these preconditions yet?<br>    a. No? *or* b. Yes? |

## WORKING IN THE
# SPIRITUAL STREAM

| Challenges | Questions for self-reflection |
|---|---|
| *To learn from other truth traditions.* | ❖ Would you consider yourself to be:<br>  a. More religious? *or*<br>  b. More spiritual?<br>❖ Are you willing to incorporate the spiritual wisdom of others into your understanding of 'the truth'?<br>  a. No? *or* b. Yes? |
| *To appreciate symbols and rituals as an expression of disclosed truth.* | ❖ Do you regard symbols and rituals as:<br>  a. Irrational? *or*<br>  b. A representation of something important about the human condition?<br>❖ Do you incorporate symbols and rituals into your own spiritual practices?<br>  a. No? *or* b. Yes? |
| *To appreciate humanity as a community of being.* | ❖ Does the word 'humanity' conjure up for you an image of:<br>  a. A collection of different peoples? *or*<br>  b. One body of all peoples?<br>❖ Is your vision for the future:<br>  a. One for you, your family and, perhaps, your community? *or*<br>  b. One for the world? |

hen you have completed this exercise, you may want to discuss your responses with a partner or trusted colleague, friend or family member. Do they recognise your self-analysis? Do they see you differently? And can they help you make sense of your own reflections in conjunction with *their* perspective of you, in order to determine which personal development challenges are most pressing for you – challenges which elicited from you an 'a' response to the associated questions above? Sense-making is always enhanced in dialogue with others: our own understanding of who we are and who we could be is invariably deepened when multiple viewpoints are shared.

Then, equipped with your conclusions, list in order of priority the three, four or, perhaps, five challenges that you know you need to address, creating thereby your personal development agenda. For example:

1. I want to be able to participate in group thinking (working in the Intellectual stream).
2. I want to be able to make distinctions about which ethical principles are the most conducive to the development of humankind (working in the Moral stream).
3. I want to understand my feelings – why particular trigger-stimuli are emotionally arousing to me (working in the Emotional stream).
4. I want to be able to cope with inner conflict (working in the Psychological stream).
5. I want to learn from other truth traditions (working in the Spiritual stream).

*V. Making the choice to move forward.*

e may know where we are now on our development journey, and we may know where we *could*
be but, unless circumstances force us forward, we
will not progress without making the choice to do
so. Researchers in the disciplines of neurobiology,
developmental psychology and education have demonstrated that
the drive to develop is innate and compelling in children and adolescents (barring organic or functional incapacity). As adults,
however, we must put ourselves *consciously* into situations in order
to learn and grow (see Chapter One). Yet the work of all the theorists demonstrates that few of us make this choice. Why is this
so? It is, of course, because we know that, in order to develop, we
need to change; and that, in order to change, we need to give up a
part of ourselves – well-established patterns of behaviour, alle-
giances, ideologies, notions of Self, or even whole lifestyles. Naturally, we are fearful of doing so, as Scott Peck explains:

"When we extend ourselves, our self enters new and unfamiliar territory, so to speak. Our self becomes a new and different self. We do things we are not accustomed to do. We change.
The experience of change, of unaccustomed activity, of being on
unfamiliar ground, of doing things differently is frightening. It
always was and always will be. People handle their fear of change
in different ways, but the fear is inescapable if they are in fact to
change."[10]

But what is the alternative? Again in the words of Peck, "the
only alternative is not to live fully or not to live at all."[11] And so, if
we do not want to number ourselves amongst the majority who,
Maslow reported, "do not amount to much", we have to find the
courage to move forward:

"Courage is not the absence of fear; it is the making of action
in spite of fear, the moving out against the resistance engendered
by fear into the unknown and into the future."[12]

As we discovered in Chapter Two, the knights who are least successful in the Grail quest are not those who fail in their adventures; they are those who have no adventures at all.[13]

### VI. Finding a guide in the modern organisation.

hen we know where we are now, *and* where we could be, *and* we have made the decision to move forward, we are ready to seek a guide. The obvious person to turn to is, of course, our boss (if we have one) given that, as we noted above, we spend most of our waking hours during our working lives in the organisation that employs us, and given, too, that all our development challenges will be manifesting themselves to some extent in the way in which we are performing our role in it. Furthermore, organisations of all types are investing heavily in the popular concept of 'leader as coach'. Coaching subordinates to solve problems and discover solutions for themselves is the mechanism which enables those who are charged with stewarding an enterprise into the future to spend less time supervising, controlling and making day-to-day decisions (increasingly hopeless activities anyway in the virtual world), and more time ensuring that their venture survives and thrives in ever more testing business circumstances.

But the reality is that our boss may not be the best guide for us on our personal learning journey: she or he may actually be behind, not ahead of us, on the human development road. In the words of Peck, "We can lead only insofar as we go before",[14] and it is a harsh but important truth that all senior executives must confront: progression through the hierarchy of an organisation is not commensurate with progression through the holarchy of personal development. Seniority and wisdom are not synonymous!

If our boss is not the right guide for us, we might turn to a professional coach. In recent years, there has been a surge in the demand for, and the provision of, professional coaching services for a number of organisational and individual reasons. For example, in the flatter, more empowered and globally distributed organisational structures of today, a 'career' is represented less as a straight-line projection from a junior role to a senior role requiring regular additions to a growing basket of skills, and more as a series of trajectories and turning points which require employees, at every juncture, to let go of old ways of doing things (their success strategy to date) in order to embrace new approaches. Professional coaches (either from outside or, increasingly, from within) are often to be found helping them to navigate these difficult turns.

At the same time, in a world in which cradle-to-grave employment is no longer offered by most organisations, employees are demanding more personally focused development support in order to maintain their employability. For many in mid-level leadership roles and above, a coach is now a non-negotiable 'must-have' to help them manage this phenomenon of the peripatetic career.

In response, a cottage industry has arisen of certification programmes and supervision schemes, to provide buyers with the reassurance they need that minimum standards of good practice are being adhered to by those who describe themselves as 'coaches'. But buyers beware. Minimum standards are seldom the mechanism for achieving

> *"Formally hired helpers are in a position to exploit and take advantage of the client and must, therefore, be limited both by formal rules and their own internal standards."*[15]
> SCHEIN

greatness. A successful helping journey is a complex, dynamic and generative relationship which occurs at the intersection of two people's life experiences, and no 'badge' of proficiency can guarantee that its owner is capable of forging these special connections.

So how, then, do we identify a *masterful* guide who can help us to address the challenges which constitute the development framework of this book? As we might expect, numerous studies have now been conducted on 'what to look for in a great coach'. Meanwhile, as I have reflected upon those who have been *my* best guides, I have found that they have certain qualities in common – qualities they share, of course, with that archetypal helper of the Arthurian legend, Merlin. I offer these observations as a contribution to the bank of information already available on the subject.

### VII. Merlin: confidant, seer, sage, strategist, kingmaker, man. (Or, The qualities of a masterful guide.)

ONFIDANT – a masterful guide can create meaningful contact with me. The coaching textbooks encourage a 'distant' relationship, a relationship between the coach and coachee which provides for a clear delineation of roles. But, as Edgar Schein observes, helpers are often not aware that their efforts to establish and maintain this sense of separateness "lead them to be so emotionally aloof that they convey an unwillingness to get involved at all."[16] So a masterful guide is someone who can create an emotionally engaged and trust-based relationship with me† which enables me to share my needs with him, knowing that they will be understood and accepted, and not used to my disadvantage.[17]

---

† *"Generously offering oneself in service to others inspires loyalty and a freedom to ask for advice and guidance."*[18] *– The Tao of Giving and Receiving Wisdom (a modern approach to mentoring which incorporates classical Taoist teachings).*

*NB The distinction between coaching and mentoring excites much angst, and many definitions have been proposed to attend to this (relatively recent) focus of concern. (The word 'coaching' only entered the English language circa 1830 whereas the word 'mentoring' derives from the name of the wise teacher, Mentor, who was asked by Odysseus to guide his son, Telemachus, as he departed Ithaca to join the Trojan war in the classical Greek epic poem, The Odyssey, attributed to Homer). The distinction between the two practices certainly has utility in some circumstances. In others, however, it may be of little consequence because masterful helpers often flex very legitimately between what may be defined conventionally as 'coaching' and what may be defined conventionally as 'mentoring'.*

EER – a masterful guide can read me. She does not just help me to reflect upon myself and make sense of the feedback I receive from others; she can also see *for herself* what I do well and what I need to do differently if I am to move ahead on my personal learning journey. (The intimacy of our relationship does not inhibit her ability to be objective, as the textbooks often assert.)

Why is this facility to 'read' me important? Well, perhaps I am embedded in the Organisational stage where I am so invested in my individuality that my ambition is preventing me from securing the commitment of those whom I lead (because no one will extend themselves simply to affirm my self-concept). Dedicated as I am to the project of 'me', I cannot view my own behaviour with detachment. In the meantime, let us assume that any feedback I am receiving from others is distorted by the lens of hierarchy or other organisational dynamics. Those below me are finding it very difficult to tell me that my conduct is preventing them from giving their best. Those above me, meanwhile, are interpreting my ambition as beneficial and actively encouraging it. (It is, after all, important for the success of the organisation that its members are ambitious both for themselves and for the whole entity; but those

THE CHINESE CHARACTER FOR 'LISTEN', *which is made up of five elements, encapsulates a method for reading another person.* EAR: *Listen for what you hear in the other person's speaking. What catches their attention? What are their priorities?* EYE: *Observe the other person. What behaviour do you notice?* HEART: *Feel the dynamic between you and him or her, recognising that you are part of that dynamic.* UNDIVIDED ATTENTION: *Let go of your prejudices and assumptions, which will otherwise influence what you hear, see, and feel.* KING: *Find a way to believe in the other person as someone who has the capability to be more effective in the manner in which they exercise their leadership.*

who are more senior than me may not see how my self-differenti-ation is translating into disaffection in those who are more junior to me.) A masterful guide will cut through whatever lip service I may pay to the importance of displaying humility (a popular mantra of current times) to see my behaviour *as it is*, and she will understand the implications of it. She will then share her obser-vations with me, allowing for the possibility, at least, that, in the words of Peck, my unconscious may reveal more to me of who I really am.[19] This ability to read me, when others around me either will not do so, or cannot do so, is a truly precious kind of seeing.

AGE – a masterful guide can lead me to a new viewpoint. He understands my world and enables me to appreciate the patterns and interdependen-cies which exist within it, so that I can interpret circumstances and events in their bigger context. When I am caught 'in the mix' of my organisational system – operating with a focus on getting things done and consumed by the day-after-day need to do more with less, with people who may not be co-located, and with an ever-expanding web of different stakeholders, all of whom are making their own, different demands of me – it can be very difficult to see it in all its whole-ness. And this fragmented perspective will only be compounded if I am still held at the level of intellectual development associated with the Organisational stage, where I may 'know' that reality is complex and multifaceted but I am, as yet, unable to *embrace* it as such.

My masterful helper, however, will guide me to a position where I will be able to 'defragment', to see the system I am respon-sible for leading in its entirety: the external forces acting upon it, the dynamics of the interactions within it, the impact it is having on its wider environment and, importantly, how I, for better or for worse through my ways of thinking, speaking and behaving, am 'calling' this continuous dance of rhythms and movement, forma-

tions and change. Previously I could only see situations to manage
– situations I did not fully understand. Now, from my new perspective, I can see futures to create – futures that I am only able
to apprehend because my helper has led me to this 'higher' viewpoint of defragmentation and insight.

TRATEGIST – a masterful guide can be in the
struggle with me. As we noted above, overcoming
a personal development challenge is a difficult and
painful (as well as a potentially transformational)
process, and I will benefit from a guide who can
walk alongside me, enabling me to wrestle with it by offering
thoughts and ideas drawn from her real-world experience of it.
So, for example, perhaps I struggle to create connection with
people (see the Social stream) and perhaps, too, I am disposition-
ally introverted (see Chapter Three). Referring to the four characteristics of mastery described so far, I need the assistance of
someone:

Confidant • Who can establish trust-based 'contact' with me.
Seer • Who understands how I relate to, adapt to, and function with,
other people now, and who can interpret and appreciate this
through the prism of my introversion.
Sage • Who understands that I need to hone my relational skills to
secure the support of those whom I lead so that, together, we
can achieve our strategic purpose in the organisation.
Strategist • Who can help me to identify the small, experimental steps – or
the "specific tasks", to use the language of Schein[20] – which will
enable me to maximise the opportunities of those social situations where I am likely to be more powerful (in more intimate
one-on-one conversations and in small groups), and also to have
a strong, visible and affinitive presence when, for example, I have
to address a large group of people (a situation in which I am
likely to be less comfortable). Someone who has, herself, grap-
pled with the same challenge of creating connection with others

and with the same preference for introversion will be particularly helpful to me here: she will know and share with me which approaches were successful for her, and which were not.

Being 'in the struggle' with me does not mean that my guide will necessarily present me with 'the answer'. In his encounters with the Dark Age Kings, Merlin frequently works in very indirect ways – by asking them questions, engaging them in dialogue, offering suggestions, speaking in riddles that they must decipher – approaches which are intended to help them discover possibilities in conjunction *with* him. Neither does being 'in the struggle' with me deny me my responsibility. I still 'own' the challenge. Only I can determine which solution will be the right one; and only I can choose to put myself into a situation where learning can occur. But it is no coincidence that the helper of our myths and legends is always old and *therefore* wise. The assistance the hero needs is the wisdom of the helper's experience. To repeat Peck's observation, "We can only lead insofar as we go before".

INGMAKER – a masterful guide can effect transformational change in me. He stays the course with me, knowing that, again in the words of Peck, "the individual trying to grow can always retreat into the easy and familiar patterns of a more limited past".[21] He continues to be available as I try to manage the fear of reinventing myself, and ensures that, when it is time for us to take our separate ways, I am a demonstrably different person from the one I was when we first began to walk together.

> "Observe calmly the natural unfolding of events.
> Rapid growth and advancement are unnatural.
> Hold to the inner vision of gradual flowering of potential.
> Avoid haste. Do not jump ahead blindly.
> Enjoy the moment of waiting to be!"[22]

ELLOW HUMAN BEING – a masterful guide can learn from me.[23] As Schein explains, the best helping relationships are equilibriated; my guide will, therefore, accord me status and importance, and will not hold me in a passive, dependent position because I need assistance. One way in which she can validate me is by being willing to learn in some way from me – by not presenting herself as the holder of all the wisdom. (The Delphic oracle described the classical philosopher, Socrates, as the wisest of men for he, alone, realised that it is only when we know that we do not know that we begin to make progress.) And it goes without saying, of course, that, by being willing to learn herself, she models the learning process for me.

hese qualities are clearly not the preserve of certificated coaches alone – indeed we are just as likely to find them in friends, colleagues, family members or even strangers, for we have, as a group-living, socially dependent species, been helping each other since *homo sapiens* first evolved. And this is, in fact, the ultimate reason the image of Merlin is so compelling as a symbol of the helper: he is a shape-shifter. As the Arthurian legend developed, he appeared in many different guises to many different people: in one text alone he is a woodcutter, a deformed herdsman, a well-dressed gentleman, an old man, a servant boy, a cripple and a reaper.† As a shape-shifter, therefore, he illustrates that help does not always present in an obvious form. It may appear, for example, in the lines of a poem, in a painting, in a piece of music, or in a story from another time and place, providing us

---

† *In Malory's* Le Morte Darthur, *in the snows of Sherwood Forest at Candlemas, Merlin appears in very strange attire:* "And Merlion was so disgysed that kynge Arthure knewe hymn nat, for he was all befurred in blacke shepis skynnes, and a grete payre of bootis, and a boowe and arowis, in a russet gowne, and brought wylde gyese in hys honed."[24]

with meaning which relates to our current life circumstances. And when it *is* available to us in the shape of another person, Merlin illustrates, through his different semblances, that no single individual can ever meet *all* our support needs, given the manifold challenges of being human (described in Chapter Two).

So how might we find this rare yet also readily available help that we require for the journey? After all, Merlin may be the principal helper of the Arthuriad, but other figures, too, offer assistance to the questing knights: skilled craftsmen construct their armour; stable boys attend to their horses; ladies of the court lace up their helmets and hauberks; squires accompany them into the forest; fellow travellers give them directions; hermits tend their wounds; boatmen ferry them across perilous rivers; noblemen provide them food and lodgings, and so on. Three simple practices are required: to be vulnerable, to be watchful and to be receptive.

*Being vulnerable* involves knowing our needs and speaking about them so that others are aware of the fact that we are seeking help. Schein observes that in certain cultures, men, in particular, find this difficult:

"The need to feel in control is especially strong in those cultures in which growing up means becoming independent, and is especially strong for males in those cultures. Being independent means you do not have to ask for help. Needing help often feels demeaning."[25]

Some words from the ancient Chinese text, *The Book of History*, may be encouraging to us all here:

"Those who seek mentoring,
   will rule the great expanse under heaven.
Those who boast that they are greater than others,
   will fall short.
Those who are willing to learn from others,
   become greater.
Those who are ego-involved,
   will be humbled and made small."[26]

*Being watchful* involves not just looking for help but noticing it when it appears – Merlin is frequently dismissed by those who are searching for him as a villain or a rogue. In the following pages, you will find a series of lists of some possible sources of support available to us, mapped against the challenges that professionals in mid-career and beyond typically face.

*Being receptive* involves pausing, listening and being willing to be disturbed. As Schein notes, receiving help is not always easy,[27] and this is certainly true when the help being offered is intended to assist us with breaking established patterns of thinking, speaking and behaving which may have served us well to date. As Schein notes, too, there is helpful help and unhelpful help,[28] but we cannot even make this distinction if we are not prepared to receive it (graciously) in the first place.

## WORKING IN THE
# INTELLECTUAL STREAM

| *Typical development challenges* | *Possible sources of help* |
|---|---|
| *If you want to see reality as compound and multifaceted, to unite and integrate ideas, and to embrace ambiguity, uncertainty and flux…* | ❖ People who challenge your thinking.<br>❖ People who are curious – who actively seek to learn from others.<br>❖ People who can elevate their thinking to see the 'wholeness' of things.<br>❖ People who can resolve seemingly incompatible alternatives.<br>❖ People whom you respect for their creativity or originality.<br>❖ People who are energised rather than thwarted by ambiguity, uncertainty and flux. |
| *If you want to participate in group thinking…* | ❖ People who have engaged in deep dialogue sessions.<br>❖ People who facilitate group thinking and problem-solving techniques.<br>❖ People who have studied native 'council' traditions and processes. |

*Some activities which may also be helpful:* Applying cognitive frameworks for understanding and working with complexity, paradox, ambiguity, uncertainty and flux; attending training programmes which employ or teach in-depth group conversational methods such as Future Search, Appreciative Inquiry, The World Café, Open Space, Dialogue and The Conference Model.

# SOCIAL STREAM

| *Typical development challenge* | *Possible sources of help* |
|---|---|
| *If you want to relate to, adapt to, and function with, other people well...* | ❖ People whom you recognise as being effective in their interpersonal relationships.<br><br>❖ Your partner, your family, your friends and trusted colleagues – people who will share 'in the moment' the impact of your interpersonal behaviour on them (so that you can learn to moderate it).<br><br>❖ People who are selected to be members of teams or projects, not for what they do but for how they work with others. |

*An activity which may also be helpful*: Participating in a Human Interaction Laboratory with the NTL Institute for Applied Behavioural Science.

WORKING IN THE
# MORAL STREAM

| Typical development challenges | Possible sources of help |
|---|---|
| *If you want to understand your own reference group's definition of 'right' and 'wrong' in terms of the many definitions available...* | ❖ People who do not choose to be defined by their cultural background.<br>❖ People who have travelled to other countries and continents and demonstrably incorporated what they have experienced into their personal philosophy.<br>❖ People who have different definitions of what is 'right' and what is 'wrong' to yours.<br>❖ Respected anthropologists, environmental specialists, historians and sociologists. |
| *If you want to make distinctions about which ethical principles are the most conducive to the development of humankind...* | ❖ People whose work is in service of the development of humankind such as peace negotiators and humanitarian aid workers with extensive experience in the field. |
| *If you want to formulate a set of self-chosen ethical principles and be willing to disobey unjust rules to defend them...* | ❖ Humanist philosophers.<br>❖ People who have put themselves at personal risk in order to defend their ethical principles. |

*Some activities which may also be helpful*: Reading the charters of global organisations, e.g. the United Nations and the World Health Organisation; participating in projects in your organisation which extend beyond geographical boundaries and challenge norms relating to how things should be accomplished; participating in environmental projects; undertaking voluntary work in areas of deprivation; reading philosophy and the biographies or autobiographies of people who have put themselves at personal risk in order to defend their ethical principles.

WORKING IN THE
# EMOTIONAL STREAM

| Typical development challenges | Possible sources of help |
| --- | --- |
| *If you want to be able to recognise your feelings…* | ❖ Your partner, colleagues, family members or friends – people who will tell you if they believe you could express your positive and/or your negative emotions more constructively. |
| *If you want to be able to understand your feelings…* | ❖ A therapist who is skilled in helping people to identify their emotional 'triggers'. |
| *If you want to be able to control maladaptive bodily responses to trigger-stimuli…* | ❖ A therapist who is skilled in helping people to direct their emotional energy effectively. |
| *If you want to be able to select appropriate responses to trigger-stimuli consciously…* | ❖ People whom you recognise as being able to manage their emotions 'with intelligence'. |

*An activity which may also be helpful*: Reading material on 'emotional intelligence'.

WORKING IN THE
# PSYCHOLOGICAL STREAM

| Typical development challenges | Possible sources of help |
| --- | --- |
| *If you want to respect the individuality of Self and others...* | ❖ People who engage in introspective practices. <br> ❖ People whom you recognise as 'growing' – individuals who are demonstrably different from the people they were in the past. <br> ❖ People who can tell 'the story' of who they are. |
| *If you want to forge relationships of interdependence...* | ❖ People who grant you your individuality in their relationships with you. |
| *If you want to cope with inner conflict...* | ❖ People who have had to make difficult personal choices. <br> ❖ Counsellors who are trained to help people make difficult choices. |
| *If you want to be interested in personal development and to concern yourself more with self-fulfilment than achievement...* | ❖ People who dedicate considerable time, effort and resources to their personal (as distinct from their professional) development. <br> ❖ A more senior person who is 'bigger' than his or her organisational role. <br> ❖ People who know what their life's work is. |
| *If you want to achieve a consolidated sense of identity (i.e. become 'self-actualised')...* | ❖ People who have done the personal work to enable them to make this shift – those rare individuals who have, recognisably, achieved this position. |

*Some activities which may also be helpful*: Journalling; 360-degree feedback processes; attending a weekend retreat; reading biographies, autobiographies and literary works in which the protagonists have overcome great personal challenges; reading material on 'self-actualisation'; attending self-development programmes.

WORKING IN THE
# SPIRITUAL STREAM

| *Typical development challenges* | *Possible sources of help* |
| --- | --- |
| *If you want to learn from other truth traditions…* | ❖ People who describe themselves as 'religious'; others who describe themselves as 'spiritual'.<br><br>❖ People who are of truth traditions which are different from your own. |
| *If you want to learn to appreciate symbols and rituals as an expression of disclosed truth…* | ❖ People who can explain the meaning of *their* symbols and traditions. |
| *If you want to appreciate humanity as a community of being…* | ❖ Spiritual guides. |

*Some activities which may also be helpful:* Visiting places of worship; reading material on the wisdom of other truth traditions; meditating.

## VIII. Conclusion.

elp we need, then, and help we can find. All our efforts may yet come to nothing, though, if we do not have an appropriate development environment for our growth, as we shall discover in the next chapter. But, before we move on, let us summarise this chapter with some additions to our rules of the road:

### The rules of the road.

1. The human development journey begins in infancy and, if growth continues, may extend into late adulthood and even until death (some, of course, may say that it extends beyond death).

2. The path that we, as travellers, follow is one of many distinct stages, each of which represents a clear, qualitative transformation of thinking and being.

3. The strengths of one stage ultimately become its limitations, a realisation which nudges us to the next stage of our growth.

4. We progress from one stage to the next by the agency of two fundamental capacities: transcendence and inclusion.

5. Research has consistently demonstrated that these stages cannot be bypassed without some compromise.

6. Each stage of the journey offers a new set of challenges (intellectual, social, moral, emotional, psychological and even spiritual challenges) which flow as streams of development through the basic stages of development.

7. These streams unfold as the stages unfold, by the same agencies of transcendence and inclusion, and also with their own dynamic.

8. If, in our determination to press onwards, we choose not to confront all the challenges available to us in the streams of development, we will arrive at the next stage of our development with some of our potential unrealised, with an imbalance in our sphere of total capability.

9. To function as a fully integrated Self, therefore, we must recognise our development gaps and then seek out those stream-specific learning experiences which will enable us to attend to them.

10. How we embrace these learning experiences will be influenced, in some measure, by our own personality.

11. The more we understand our personality, the more we understand the behavioural choices available to us.

12. Knowing when and how to act 'in character' and when and how to act 'out of character' – whilst still being authentic – equips us to be more effective in a wider and wider range of situations.

13. In order to move forward on our development pathway, however, we must be willing to change; and, in order to change, we must be willing to give up a part of ourselves which, naturally, evokes fear in us, and calls for courage.

14. Happily we are not travelling alone: guides for the journey are available whenever a daunting challenge arises.

15. Masterful guides are those who can create meaningful contact with us, who can read us, who can lead us to a new viewpoint, who can be in the struggle with us, who can effect transformational change in us, and who can also learn from us.

16. If we are willing to be vulnerable, watchful and receptive, we will find the help we need.

# FINDING
# MERLIN

## THE *FOREST* OF
# ADVENTURE

*And he rode back along the path that he thought would take him to the house of his grandfather the Fisher King; but he was way off the track, and rode on in great dejection. Two days and nights he rode, with nothing to eat except apples and other fruit he found in the forest...*

Robert de Boron[1]

PERCEVAL

# The Forest of Adventure

*I. The forest as a holding environment.*

ing Arthur's knights ride out from the court to seek their adventures in the surrounding forest. But the forest is not simply a convenient location for their exploits: it provides all the conditions the questing warriors need – food, shelter and a myriad of helpful hermits, as well as the now familiar stock of wrathful villains and fearsome beasts to test their worth. The medieval storytellers were very aware of how essential our environment is to us as the venue for our growth.

Modern theorists have also emphasised the critical role that our environment plays. Robert Kegan, for example, influenced by the ideas of Sigmund Freud, Jean Piaget, Erik Erikson and Donald W. Winnicott, notes that:

"As important as it is to understand the way the person creates the world, we must also understand the way the world creates the person."[2]

Each stage of development, Kegan explains, requires its own 'holding' environment. This culturing context does not keep or confine the individual at his current developmental stage but serves three special functions:

First, the environment, like a crucible, *holds* the individual, enabling him to become embedded in his current stage and confirming him, therefore, in this achievement. At this point, he is effectively *fused* with his culturing context.

Secondly, the environment *lets go* of him as he emerges from his state of embeddedness, enabling him to explore safely to the edge of his present limits. It recognises and promotes this process of emergence so that the individual can then redefine his relationship to the culture as something to which he is no longer fused but to which he now *relates*.

And, thirdly, as he moves on to attain a new state of equilibrium, the environment *remains in place* safeguarding his transition to his new developmental stage by being available should the safety and security it affords be temporarily required. At this point, the individual can again redefine his relationship to the culture: now it is something from which he has *separated*. This act of separation enables him to fuse with a new holding environment which, though it will be shaped in some measure by the old one, must also be substantially different, for it has to serve as the crucible for his new and different state of equilibrium.

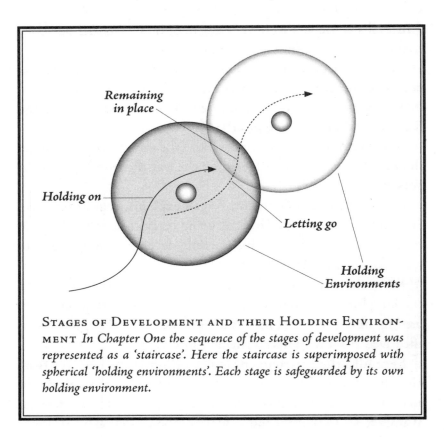

*Remaining in place*

*Holding on*

*Letting go*

*Holding Environments*

STAGES OF DEVELOPMENT AND THEIR HOLDING ENVIRON-MENT *In Chapter One the sequence of the stages of development was represented as a 'staircase'. Here the staircase is superimposed with spherical 'holding environments'. Each stage is safeguarded by its own holding environment.*

## II. The holding environments of the human development journey.

rawing upon the work of a number of scholars, researchers and theorists, and notably that of Kevin Durkin, I describe here the different culturing contexts which support a person's progress along the human development road. I suggest the likely consequences for those who suffer the misfortune of being deprived of these important venues; and I also emphasise the responsibility that adults have, as custodians of them, to ensure that they are in place for all those within their social milieu who are reliant upon them for their growth. Specifically, I invite readers who maintain the development ground of their organisation (chief executives, organisational leaders, members of boards of directors, organisation development practitioners, human resource professionals, learning and development specialists, and talent and capability managers, for example) to consider whether or not you are providing the culturing context which will enable members to progress to the World-Centric stage and live there with all the functional maturity of a fully integrated Self – for the organisation, as the place where most of us spend most of our waking hours until we retire, is the primary venue for growth in adulthood.

### III. The first holding environment: the primary caregiving matrix.

uring my infancy, my "warm, intimate and continuous relationship"[3] with my primary caregivers is the culturing context in which I become embedded in, then emerge from, and then move on from, the Sensorimotor stage of my development. (Many of the early investigators and theorists, following the pioneering researcher, John Bowlby, assumed that the primary relationships that infants construct are singular and monotropic, i.e.

that they are formed between infants and their biological mothers only. Subsequent research in modern family structures has revealed that infants are capable of forming several primary relationships, and that the first one may be with their father.[4])

### III. a. Holding on, letting go and remaining in place.

o, initially, my environment 'holds' me – both literally and metaphorically – as a newly born, undifferentiated Self in my fusion with the physical world. As we noted in the description of the Social stream, I am well equipped to promote these first connections with my disproportionately large eyes and head-to-body ratio which are arousing to adults. My parents really enjoy the physical contact of their close proximity to me.

Then, at seven to eleven months, as I discover that I am a separate Self and that so, too, is 'the other', my relationships with my primary caregivers become 'securely attached' (see, again, the Social stream), fostering in me the foundational capacity for empathy – to understand what 'the other' is experiencing and to respond appropriately.

With secure attachments in place, my holding environment can now, in an apparent contradiction, 'let go' of me. 'Letting go' in this sense means that my parents encourage me to move out from my secure base (my close proximity to them) to investigate, and experiment with, new things and new 'others'[5]; and this I do inquisitively and confidently because I know I can return to them for comfort and reassurance if I perceive a threat.

Then, having held me, and let go of me, my caregivers 'remain in place' as I move on to identify with the next stage of my growth, the Impulsive stage. They are still accessible to me when I need them *and* they also evolve with me to become part of a bigger culture – my family – which will be the crucible for my embeddedness in my new and different state of equilibrium.

### III. b. What if this first holding environment is not available?

esearch demonstrates that if my parents fail to create a "warm, intimate and continuous relationship" with me at the Sensorimotor stage, with the result that I fail to become securely attached to at least one of them, my ability to create attachments generally, perhaps for years to come, may be compromised. This is of great consequence because relationships are, fundamentally, developmental – much of the progress I am able to make through all the streams of development must occur, necessarily, within them (see Chapter Two). In the meantime, without a secure base to explore and learn from, I will be reluctant to discover new toys and interact with new people. Studies indicate that I am, therefore, likely to be disadvantaged in comparison with securely attached children in terms of autonomy, interpersonal competence and willingness to learn during my toddler, pre-school and early school years.[6]

### III. c. The responsibility of the adult.

s Durkin explains,[7] it is still not clear which aspects of parental behaviour are important for establishing attachment relationships, although sensitivity to the infant and the harmony of the customary interaction style have been associated with the formation of secure connections; and highly stressed, abusive and neglectful contexts have been associated with the formation of insecure connections. Notwithstanding this lack of clarity, it is obvious that my responsibility as an adult is to ensure that, with any child whom I parent, I do all I can to create the conditions in which secure attachments can form and thrive.

Then, at the right time, I must 'let go'. As Kegan explains,[8] a parent who 'holds on' too firmly, who will not allow a child to explore and learn, who wants, in some way, to keep him as a baby, is denying him the possibility of differentiation and of developing personal independence.

And, finally, I must continue to be available to my toddlers, to be the bridge between the old environment and the new as they become embedded in the next state of equilibrium, the Impulsive stage, so that they can successfully integrate the achievements of the Sensorimotor stage into their new sense of Self.

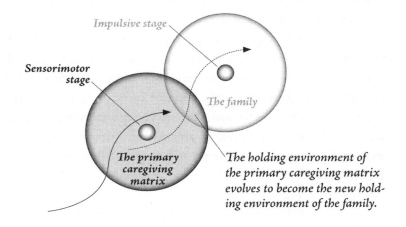

The holding environment of the primary caregiving matrix evolves to become the new holding environment of the family.

## IV. The second holding environment: the family.

uring my pre-school years, as noted above, my primary caregivers evolve to be significant participants in my new holding environment although other family members, my siblings, and age-mates whom my parents select especially for me, are now part of my culturing context, too, as I become embedded in, then emerge from, and then move on from, my newly found purposes and perceptions, which are the hallmark of the Impulsive stage.

*IV. a. Holding on, letting go and remaining in place.*

y siblings and age-mates join in pretend play with me, which fosters me in my all-important whims and fantasies, affirming thereby my sense of a separate identity. My adult relatives, whilst they set boundaries to constrain my more extreme impulses, also enjoy playing with me and participating in my magical thinking by, for example, leaving presents for me from Santa and coins under my pillow from the Tooth Fairy in Western cultures.

But, between the ages of five and seven, as I develop a self-concept (a sense of *what* I am as opposed to my earlier sense *that* I am), I begin to separate myself from my purposes and perceptions, and so my holding environment lets go of me (for, as Durkin reports, the family is a constantly evolving unit, reorganising itself as a result of developmental changes in me[9]). My parents now expect me to learn to regulate my impulses – to sleep in my own bed at night, to dress myself as fully as possible and to try to clean my teeth – so that I can assume an authority for myself, in preparation for my entry into the wider world.

Then, having held me, and let go of me, my family members remain in place as I move on to identify with the next stage of my growth, the Imperial stage. They are still accessible to me when I need them *and* they also evolve with me to become part of a bigger culture, a wider milieu of my relatives, friends and teachers. This culture will be the crucible for my embeddedness in my new and different state of equilibrium.

*IV. b. What if this second holding environment is not available?*

sychologists are very interested in families, of course, and three parenting styles have been identified (organised on two dimensions of emotional responsiveness and control/demandingness) to describe the relationship between social context and child development: Authoritarian, Authoritative and Permissive.[10] Negative outcomes are to be expected for my overall development if my adult family members have an authoritarian parenting style – who obtain low scores on measures of warmth and responsiveness and high scores on measures of control; and who are, therefore, intolerant of my 'childish' impulses, setting high maturity demands of me. Negative outcomes are also to be expected if I experience a permissive parenting style from adult family members – who have a high level of tolerance for my impulses and who obtain low scores on control, exercising little constraining influence over me, even when necessary.

### IV. c. The responsibility of the adult.

 number of factors influence parenting orientations, including the ideological values of both the parents and the society in which they live, their economic circumstances, their personality, the personality of their children, and the level of accord or discord in their (marital) relationship.[11] Notwithstanding this multiplicity of factors which must be managed, it is clear that my responsibility as an adult is to ensure that, with any young children in my family unit, I do all I can to support the fulfilment of their impulses, containing them only when necessary; and that I also take the very enjoyable opportunities which present to join with them in their magical world.

Then, at the right time, I must let go by promoting their movement towards self-sufficiency in order to prepare them for attending school. Over-involvement on my part in their impulses will have consequences which are likely to be many and serious. Children who are 'stranded' in their own purposes and perceptions will not be ready for the psychological tasks of the classroom and the playground. In addition, more mature age-mates are likely to recognise them as somehow 'different' and ostracise them from the peer group (a context which is, of course, very important for development in middle childhood).

And, finally, I must continue to be available to them, to be the bridge between the old environment and the new as they become embedded in the next state of equilibrium, the Imperial stage, so that they can successfully integrate the achievements of the Impulsive stage into their new sense of Self.

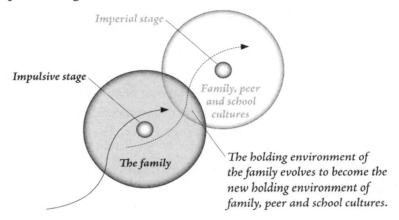

The holding environment of the family evolves to become the new holding environment of family, peer and school cultures.

### V. The third holding environment: family, peer and school cultures.

 s noted above, during my middle childhood years, and with a sense of *'what* I am', my relatives, together with my friends and teachers, evolve to be participants in my new holding environment as I become embedded in, then emerge from, and then move on from, my own needs, interests and wishes which are the hallmark of the Imperial stage.

### V. a. Holding on, letting go and remaining in place.

 y central task at the Imperial stage is to display, test and confirm my just-discovered, self-centred, self-asserting and self-determining concept of 'me'. My family is an important venue for this activity: my parents, grandparents, aunts and uncles listen to me read, admire my artwork, and applaud me for my accomplishments on the sports field and in the summer con-

cert. My peer group, which I form with others who are 'similar' to me (according to factors such as my neighbourhood, my social class, my ethnicity, my language and, perhaps, my gender[12]), is another venue for me to display my new Self. And so, too, is my formal school culture: sensitive teachers will not shame or humiliate me for my mistakes, especially in front of the whole class!

But, as I approach adolescence and begin to separate myself from my personal needs, interests and wishes, my holding environment lets go of me. My relatives, friends and teachers make me aware that my self-centred behaviour is no longer tolerable. I am now required to co-ordinate my concerns with the concerns of others – to take their feelings into account, to keep commitments, and to meet expectations.

And then, having held me and let go of me, my relatives, friends and teachers remain in place for me as I move on to identify with the next stage of my growth, the Relational stage. They are available to me when I need them *and* they also evolve with me to become part of a bigger culture, my interpersonal relationships with people in my expanding social world. This culture will be the crucible for my embeddedness in my new and different state of equilibrium.

### V. b. What if this third holding environment is not available?

any specialists in child development have demonstrated that the non-involvement of adult family members in my middle childhood is likely to have negative consequences for me as I strive to affirm my self-concept. Scott Peck in fact challenges *all* parents to spend more time with their offspring during these formative years:

"When we love something it is of value to us, and when something is of value to us we spend time with it, time enjoying it and time taking care of it…. So it is when we love children; we spend time admiring them and caring for them… [and] when children have learned through the love of their parents to feel valuable, it is almost impossible for the vicissitudes of adulthood to destroy their spirit."[13]

Given the importance of the peer group for my growth in my middle childhood, it is also obvious that there are potential liabilities to me if I am not successful in making and sustaining friendships because these interactions are not only vehicles for display.[14] Research illustrates that their affective functions include fostering the growth of social competence; serving as sources of ego support, intimacy and affection; and providing companionship, stimulation, guidance, assistance, a sense of reliable reliance, and also emotional security in novel or potentially threatening situations.[15] As a young child is emerging from the familiarity and security of family life into the wider world, the comfort, reassurance and direction they offer are of great relevance; and if I am unable to participate in them I will certainly be disadvantaged as I seek to test and confirm my sense of 'what I am'. And if I am unfortunate enough to have teachers who do not arrange opportunities for me to prove myself in my formal school culture, my progress will also, self-evidently, be compromised.

### V. c. The responsibility of the adult.

dults continue to play an important role in creating an appropriate development environment for middle childhood, notwithstanding the salience of peer relations. As such, it is my responsibility to ensure that I affirm the emerging self-construct of all imperial-stage children within my social milieu by acknowledging and endorsing their achievements. If I see them struggling to be accepted by their peers, I must help them to choose friends who *can* become their 'group', and guide them to behave in such a way that it becomes possible for them to be part of it. In addition, I must verify that their formal school culture is also supporting their growth by enabling them to succeed in as many activities as possible there.

Then, at the right time, I must let go by making clear to them that their imperial way of organising their world is no longer tolerable, and that they must now co-ordinate their concerns with those of others. My over-involvement in their self-aggrandisement will limit their ability to orientate themselves towards mutuality and, therefore, to construct those interpersonal relationships which are the primary venue for development in adolescence.

And, finally, I must continue to be available to them, to be the bridge between the old environment and the new as they become embedded in the next state of equilibrium, the Relational stage, so that they can successfully integrate the achievements of the Imperial stage into their new sense of Self.

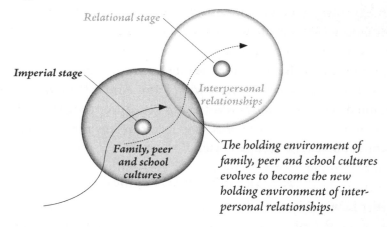

The holding environment of family, peer and school cultures evolves to become the new holding environment of interpersonal relationships.

## VI. The fourth holding environment: interpersonal relationships.

 uring my adolescent years, as noted above, my relatives, friends and teachers evolve to be significant participants in my new holding environment as I become embedded in, then emerge from, and then move on from, my relationships, the hallmark, of course, of the Relational stage. But they must undergo a material role change in order to make this transition. Adult family members and teachers must become more like friends, and my peers

must become confidants (so our peer interactions, which were formerly constructed, at least in part, to serve our individual needs, must be reconstructed for the purposes of affinity). Other relationships become salient, too, as I move out into the adult world: as Durkin reports, there is no "closed budget" on the number I may have, each of which affords a different type of interpersonal support.[16]

### VI. a. Holding on, letting go and remaining in place.

ne of my central tasks as an adolescent is to acquire a unified self-image, a sense of 'who I am' – an objective assisted by a major expansion in my reasoning capacity (see the Intellectual stream), which fosters increasing self-awareness and an appreciation of difference in others (people who are different from me and different from each other). This conscious attempt at self-definition, however, is occurring at a period in my life cycle defined by disruption, even turbulence. Biological changes are taking place as I enter puberty; I am transferring from a small, familiar setting of a junior school, where I was in the 'top class', to a large, impersonal setting of a senior school where I am in the 'bottom class'; and as the pioneering thinker in the social sciences, Kurt Lewin, observes, I am also making a momentous social shift as an individual who was a child but who is now en route to adulthood – an unknown position which I approach with many uncertainties.[17] In the context of all this disruption, Durkin asks:

"With the surge of hormones, the growth of secondary sexual characteristics, the stimulus of genital arousal, the pressures of educational and career choices, the temptations of drugs, the sway of the peer group, the conflicting messages of the mass media, the lure of Satan, suicide and debauchery in rock music, the impending trials of adulthood, the state the world is in today, the sheer social gaucheness of being 15, and the eruption of pimples – is it any wonder that adolescents sometimes freak out?"[18]

Whenever human beings are confronted with a significant life change, they naturally seek information about what is to happen, and strive to organise their understanding as events unfold.[19] During my adolescence this endeavour takes place in my conversations with those who are experiencing the same life changes as I. It is for this reason that my relationships with my peers are such an important venue for my development at this time (although they do not replace those that I have with, for example, my parents – see below). The physical meeting places of adolescence (the street, the coffee shop, the shopping mall, the sports club, the train station, the cinema and so on) also provide me with important opportunities to create a sense of personal order; in these settings my network of relationships expands to include neighbours, shopkeepers, sports coaches, youth club leaders and so on, all of whom have a role to play in my drive for self-definition.

But, in late adolescence, with a sense, at last, of who I am, and as I prepare to make my entrance into the adult world as an independent being, I begin to separate myself from my relationships, and so my holding environment lets go of me.

And then, having held me and let go of me, my relationships remain in place for me as I move on to identify with the next stage of my growth, the Organisational stage. They are available to me when I need them *and* they also evolve with me to become part of a bigger culture, organisational settings. This will be the crucible for my embeddedness in my new and different state of equilibrium.

*VI. b. What if this fourth holding environment is not available?*

 dolescents report that those whom they rate as most significant to them are core family members, especially their parents, who provide them with the psychological autonomy and behavioural regulation they need during these years of change[20]:

"Individuation is not something that happens from parents but rather with them… just as the securely attached infant is able to venture from the parental base, so the securely attached adolescent is able to address the challenges of self-determination…."[21]

If my parents, in their relationships with me, deprive me of opportunities to create a sense of personal order (i.e. they maintain excessive psychological control over me), I may be at risk of withdrawal and internalised problems such as anxiety, depression, eating disorders and even suicidal behaviour (which becomes much more common in adolescence than in earlier years, is associated with a weak sense of personal continuity and low self-esteem, and is also increasing in occurrence in developed nations across the world). Alternatively, if my parents allow me plenty of autonomy but fail to offer the behavioural guidance I need, I may be at risk of externalised problems such as early and excessive abuse of legal and illegal substances (which I may employ as a coping strategy), truancy, sexual risk-taking and general deviancy, all of which are strongly correlated. And if I have to suffer other stress factors within the family such as protracted marital discord, parental absence, substance abuse, violence, criminality, or relationships with my parents which are harsh or cruel, I may even be at risk of delinquency.[22] (Delinquency is a state which is difficult to define: research indicates that most young people will commit a criminal act such as shoplifting, vandalism or driving whilst under the influence of legal or illegal drugs. For our purposes, we can assume that the term describes sustained involvement in criminal activity.)

In all these circumstances, where my core family members are failing to construct with me the developmental relationships I need, I will, if I do not withdraw completely, turn to my peers who are, as we now know, rated as increasingly significant with age. My deviant or delinquent activities are, however, likely to exclude me from groups whose members have a high level of self-efficacy.

(As Durkin wryly observes: "Peer influence is not invariably oriented toward risk and antisocial behavior."[23]) But they will be the criteria for inclusion and credibility in others. Indeed the locus of such behaviour *is* the peer group: "actions do not take on meaning until they have an audience of like-minded others."[24] Here I can exercise the social identity I have, effectively, chosen for myself – the deviant or delinquent alternative – which is actually a *positive* choice because no alternatives in my dysfunctional environment are meaningful for me.

Of course, other relationships are salient to me in adolescence, notably those with teachers. But even the most supportive of teachers may not be able to 'reach' me in my frustrated search for identity (negative attitudes to school and delinquency correlate highly). And other adult members of society may also wish to help me but may not know how, or may be too afraid, to approach me because of my unruly behaviour.

### VI. c. *The responsibility of the adult.*

s an adult, it is my responsibility to forge friendships with all adolescents within my social milieu. I must no longer be an authority figure. I must, instead, reposition myself to help them work through the disruption of this period of change in their lives in conversations in which I grant them equal status to me.

Then, at the right time, when they have clearly developed a unified self-image, I must let go. Over-involvement in my relationships with them may lead to them being trapped at the Relational stage. (In Chapter One, we noted the desperate plight of those chronologically aged adults, who have otherwise progressed normally through the foregoing stages of development, but who do not progress from the Relational stage to the Organisational stage. Lodged in a state of emotional dependency, they continue to be needful of others, unable to define themselves as autono-

mous beings and without a sense of independent purpose.) Conflicts often arise in families at this point, as the young person's
need to express his or her autonomy clashes with the parents'
sense of responsibility for their son or daughter.[25] But if I can
appreciate such clashes for what they are – predictable events in
the process of 'letting go' – I can orientate myself constructively
towards them.

And, finally, I must continue to maintain my friendships with
the adolescents in my acquaintance as they become embedded in
the next state of equilibrium, the Organisational stage, enabling
them to integrate successfully the achievements of the Relational
stage into their new sense of Self:

"It takes a special wisdom for the family of an adolescent to
understand that by remaining in place so that the adolescent can
have the family there to ignore and reject, the family is providing
something very important, and is still, in a new way, intimately
and importantly involved in the child's development. This special
wisdom is intrinsic to many families, and its source is derived not
from psychological experts but from nature itself."[26]

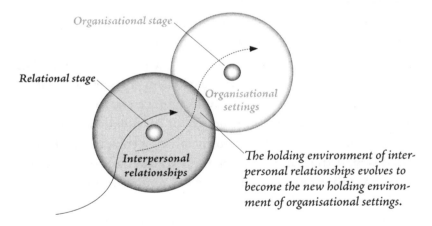

Organisational stage

Relational stage

Organisational
settings

Interpersonal
relationships

The holding environment of interpersonal relationships evolves to
become the new holding environment of organisational settings.

### VII. *The fifth holding environment:*
### *organisational settings.*

uring my late teens and early twenties my relationships continue to be important elements of my new holding environment as I become embedded in my autonomous Selfhood, the hallmark of the Organisational stage. But those with whom I have these relationships allow them to be relativised or placed in the bigger context of my self-authorship – for now, in the words of Kegan, I have the capacity to sustain myself, to parent myself, to name myself.[27]

### VII. a. *The organisation as a venue which holds me so that*
### *I can be the person I have become.*

central task of my young adulthood is to obtain group recognition of my just-discovered individuality and, as I enter the workforce to secure economic independence, my organisation – whether it be in the private, public or not-for-profit sector – will be well suited to providing me with a venue in which I can achieve this purpose. My ideology meshes with *its* ideology, and its structured and regularised context (its architecture of roles, responsibilities and reporting relationships; its well-tested and well-documented policies, procedures, processes and practices; its focus on delivering proven products or services to a known customer base; and its orientation to solving problems in the here-and-now) fosters me, too, in my exercises of self-discipline, personal achievement, pride in myself and ambition. This is an environment in which I can immerse myself fully because it is the place in which I am able to be the person I have *become*.

### VII. b. What if this environment is not available to me?

s Durkin explains, developmental changes in self-understanding and self-definition in adolescence are reflected in the emergence of a 'vocational self-concept', which is influenced by a number of factors including socio-economic circumstances:

"It helps to come from a stable, affluent, affectionate, cognitively stimulating home with educationally aware parents. Adolescents from lower socio-economic families aspire to relatively low-status occupations while those from middle-class backgrounds set their sights higher."[28]

The parenting style I experienced (*authoritative* parenting fosters high levels of educational performance), my 'future time perspective' (my awareness of the structure of the future and the relationship between current activities and choices and later outcomes[29]), the aspirations of my parents (which guide my expectations about my future) and shared norms about what the future might hold within my peer group also have a bearing.[30] If any or all of these factors limit my particular vocational self-concept with the result that the form of employment I secure as a young adult is not stimulating, I may develop a reduced self-image, a low sense of self-efficacy and other maladjustments including depression. I face these risks, too, if I have a strong vocational self-concept but enter the workforce during a period of economic recession, when career opportunities (rather than job opportunities) are constrained, and low-status or low-skilled jobs are the only means of earning a living. And if I am unable to find any form of employment for a protracted period of time I can expect to suffer significant psychological distress, as numerous studies of the effect of unemployment have demonstrated, because this experience is actually preventing me from entering the adult world.[31]

### VII. c. The responsibility of the adult.

s an adult, my responsibility towards all young people within my social milieu is to support them in their efforts to find suitable employment. And if I serve an organisation as, for example, a chief executive, an organisational leader, a member of the board of directors, an organisation development practitioner, a human resource professional, a learning and development specialist, or a talent and capability manager, it is also my responsibility to provide a holding environment in the workplace which will enable them to exercise fully their new-found autonomy. It does, of course, make good business sense for me to do so. But, at the right time, I must also let go of them, along with all organisational-stage employees, and provide them with a different holding environment which will enable them to progress to the World-Centric stage.

Why, though, would I choose to do this? Members who are held at the Organisational stage are serving the enterprise very effectively. They know their place in the hierarchy, they defer to those more senior than themselves, and they understand their role – what they are expected to do and by when. They function relatively independently and take pride in their work, so they can be relied upon to deliver to a high standard. They oversee those beneath them, ensuring they, too, deliver to a high standard. And they are demonstrably committed to the enterprise – so they conform to the cultural expectations of it, they represent it favourably to the outside world, and they are ambitious for its success as well as for their own, for they know that the two are inextricably linked. They are, in other words, loyal servants of the organisation-as-is. So why would it make sense for me, with the organisation's interests in mind, to dedicate time, effort and resources to nurture the growth of employees to a higher stage of development?

The reason is that a holding environment which fosters the autonomous ways of thinking and being which characterise the Organisational stage necessarily limits the ability of people and the enterprise (the development of which are interdependent, as we shall discover in the Conclusion to this book) to achieve their fullest potential. This has implications for all: for the members themselves, for the enterprise, and for the wider community.

Organisations are operating today in a world of interconnectedness, as Louise Diamond explains:

"Our thought leaders and those able to see the bigger picture tell us we are living in a time of profound paradigm shift similar to our leap from agricultural to industrial societies. We are moving from a world of separation to a world of interconnectedness; from a mechanistic or reductionist worldview to a holistic or quantum understanding of the nature of reality; from a world of industrial growth that depletes to a world of sustainability that replenishes."[32]†

And, yet, they are also operating in a world which is riven by climate change, economic crises, scarcity of water and other

† *During the late nineteenth and early twentieth centuries, classical Newtonian physics struggled to explain certain phenomena and experimental observations, despite its high level of utility in describing and predicting the everyday behaviour of the natural world. The theoretical edifice of an objective reality (informed originally by the great empirical enquirers of the seventeenth-century Enlightenment) began to crumble as the physicist, Sir John Polkinghorne, explains:*

*"What had been considered to be the arena of clear and determinate process was found to be, at its subatomic roots, cloudy and fitful in its behaviour."[33]*

*Strange and surprising quantum ideas of non-locality, mutual influence, indeterminacy, and instantaneous and discontinuous change were proposed.*

*"As Bohr [the Nobel prize-winning physicist] once said, the world is not only stranger than we thought; it is stranger than we could think."[34]*

*And these new insights now inform the philosophical backcloth against which organisations are grappling with the multiple crises of our globalised world (see the account of 'Changing Theories of Organisational Change' provided by Robert J. Marshak on the following pages).*

*Changing theories of organisational change.*

obert J. Marshak, scholar in applied behavioural science, describes four main influences on how change is conceptualised in organisations in the practice of Organisation Development.

"One is based on the mechanical sciences and implies organisations are closed, determinate systems with productivity and efficiency as primary criteria and where changes are needed to 'fix' or 're-engineer' some process or function, especially when 'broken.' Another is based on the biological sciences and views organisations as contingent, open systems. Alignment, congruence and successful strategic positioning of the organisation become key criteria and change is needed when the organisation must adapt or re-position itself given changes in its environment. These two ways of thinking about organisations dominated organisation and management theory in the first sixty to seventy years of the last century. They, especially open systems theory, were the dominant theories when Organisation Development was first formulated and both helped shape Organisation Development thinking about the whats, whys and hows of organisational change in the foundational years of the late 1950s to the late 1970s.

"These ways of thinking about organisations and change have continued to shape Organisation Development theory and practice into the new century, but have been augmented by two newer ways of thinking since about the 1980s. A range of ideas linked to social construction, meaning-making, organisation culture, and the role of language, conversation, and discourse, among others, are loosely bundled here as part of what I am calling the interpretive sciences. Instead of assuming an objective reality to be discovered or discerned, the interpretive sciences view organisations as generative, meaning-making systems where participants are actively involved in the social construction and re-construction of their reality. The current popular interest in changing the conversation as a primary way to achieve organisational change is a reflection of this way of thinking. Change is a function of asking different questions or reframing and/or renaming organisational phenomena. Another stream of thinking originating in physics, but gaining prominence in the social sciences in the 1990s, directly addresses change and change theory. Drawing on chaos and complexity theory, organisations are conceived of as complex, adaptive systems. Instead of planned, episodic change, these newer ideas suggest that change can be both continuous and self-organising. Consequently, start-stop ways of thinking about change are replaced with ideas about facilitating minimally bounded processes of re-creation and transformation; staying with the flux and flow of things while fostering the emergence of new possibilities at the edge of chaos."[35]

| Source: | Mechanical Sciences *1900s to the present* | Biological Sciences *1960s to the present* | Interpretive Sciences *1980s to the present* | Complexity Sciences *1990s to the present* |
|---|---|---|---|---|
| Organisa-tions are: | Determinate, closed systems | Contingent, open systems | Generative, meaning-making systems | Complex, adaptive systems |
| Focus on: | Efficiency, plans, structure, IT, productivity | Alignment, congruence, strategic plans | Discourse, culture, meaning-making, consciousness | Chaos, self-organisation, emergent design |
| Change by: | Fix and re-engineer | Adapt and re-position | Reframe and rename | Flux and emergence |

resources, hunger, war, criminality, terrorism and man-made disasters in addition to natural catastrophes. In previous times, the threats experienced by human societies were local threats requiring local solutions. In our globalised community, one in which our political, economic, social, climatic and environmental systems are failing simultaneously, the threats we face as an interrelated and interdependent human species charged with the guardianship of a planet we share with every other living species, are of an existential magnitude.

However, from complexity theory (the study of complex, adaptive systems), we learn that:

"...it is precisely at that edge of chaos that the greatest opportunity for creative change exists. When failing systems reach a certain degree of instability, the opportunity arises for innovative solutions and new ideas to emerge. Breakdown calls out for breakthrough; systemic failures call for systems transformation."[36]

Organisations, as essential elements of our interconnected world, are obligated to play their part in this important work of system transformation (to safeguard their own survival, incidentally, as well as that of the wider community). But, to do so, a new way of thinking (and, therefore, of being) – which is not of the level of consciousness that gave rise to these multiple crises – is required of their members. This new way of thinking is, of course, the holistic, integral mode of meaning-making which is only available to us when we have reached the World-Centric stage, as will be apparent if we remind ourselves again of the developmental achievements of this stage and how they may be demonstrated in our organisational lives.

> *"Suddenly we understand that truly we are all in this together, and that the boundaries of nation state, individual well-being, and national security are superseded by the transnational flow of information, goods, people, money, and the need to address the well-being of the whole."*[37]

# WORLD-CENTRIC STAGE
## A REMINDER

### THE POSITION OF THE WORLD-CENTRIC STAGE

At last I can embrace a truly global perspective: my group
is not the only group in the universe!

### PRINCIPAL STREAM-RELATED ACHIEVEMENTS

*Intellectual:* Conceptual sophistication (enabling oneself, for
example, to engage in subjective, interpersonal and
non-rational thought processes, and to embrace
complexity, paradox, ambiguity, uncertainty and
flux). Then, in time, the capacity to participate in
group thinking.

*Social:* Full social competence, i.e. the ability to relate to,
adapt to, and function with, other people.

*Moral:* The definition of an action as 'right' or 'wrong'
according to whether or not it makes for a good
society (this requires a recognition that one's own
reference group's definition of 'right' and 'wrong' is
only one among many, plus a preparedness to make
distinctions about which ethical principles are the
most conducive to the development of humankind).
Then, in time, self-chosen ethical principles and a
preparedness to take action to defend them.

*Emotional:* Full emotional competence, i.e. the ability to
recognise the specific feelings that trigger-stimuli
arouse in oneself; to understand those feelings (why
the stimuli are emotionally arousing to oneself);
to control maladaptive bodily responses; and to
select, consciously, appropriate responses to those
stimuli.

*(continued overleaf)*

# WORLD-CENTRIC STAGE
## A REMINDER

### PRINCIPAL STREAM-RELATED ACHIEVEMENTS (CONT'D)

*Psychological:* Respect for individuality (that of Self and others); relationships of interdependence; the ability to cope with inner conflict; an interest in one's own development and a goal of self-fulfilment (partly supplanting achievement). Then, in time, a consolidated sense of identity, i.e. 'self-actualisation'.

*Spiritual:* Significant encounters with other truth traditions; renewed appreciation of those symbols and rituals which are the expression of disclosed truth; the awareness of humanity as an inclusive community of being.

### HOW THE ACHIEVEMENTS OF THIS STAGE MAY BE DEMONSTRATED IN OUR ORGANISATIONAL LIVES

*At the intra-personal level I can:*

1. Pursue self-fulfilment rather than achievement, because I have now separated myself from my activities, whereas I defined myself by them at the former Organisational stage.
2. Give up my certainty for curiosity because 'not knowing' is now a state which does not threaten my sense of who I am.
3. Embrace complexity, paradox, ambiguity, uncertainty and flux because I now know that reality is not defined by my wishes, hopes, fears, anxieties, theories and beliefs, or those of my cultural group.
4. Tolerate the shortcomings of myself and others because I now accept human nature for what it is rather than how I would prefer it to be.
5. Acknowledge and cope with the inner conflicts I feel – between conflicting needs, conflicting duties, and the conflict between needs and duties (at work, in life, and between work and life) – because I now understand that they are part of the human condition and I have the courage to deal with them as such.

# WORLD-CENTRIC STAGE
## A REMINDER

*At the inter-individual level I can:*

1. Learn from anyone who can teach me because I have now renounced my socio-centric stance.
2. Experience deep feelings of connection with, and empathy for, other people because I now realise that we all belong to the same human family.
3. Forge profound, interdependent relationships with them because I now respect, and grant them, their own individuality.
4. Manage my ongoing interactions with them as a complex but fluent series of interpersonal negotiations because my relationships are now important to me for their own sake.
5. Express positive and negative emotions constructively because I now appreciate how my behaviour may create, disrupt or even destroy these relationships.

*At the organisational level I can:*

1. Challenge 'business as usual' and find creative solutions to problems because now I am not invested in the preservation of my organisation as-it-is as the venue in which I affirm my identity.
2. Evaluate the effect that the organisation is having on the local community, the natural environment, the nation and the world because I now perceive it in the context of the wider system in which it operates.
3. Advance an international rather than a merely multi-national position because I now understand the meaning of a globalised (i.e. an interrelated and interdependent) world.
4. Advocate and defend strong, self-chosen ethical principles in the exercise of my leadership because my moral perspective is now a concern for the welfare of all humankind.
5. Propose a greater purpose for the organisation than to exist simply to maintain itself because I am now able to envision the role it could play in the world.

### VIII. Conclusion.

o, it certainly does make good business sense for an organisation, as the place where its members spend most of their waking hours and as, therefore, their primary container for growth, to provide a culturing context which will nurture them to the World-Centric stage and 'hold' them as they become embedded there. If it does do so, it will be offering a venue in which people can give up their individuality, separate themselves from their activities, and renounce their socio-centric stance, enabling them, thereby, to make their fullest contribution – learning from each other, working in relationship with each other, and finding creative solutions to problems with each other. Then, with a critical mass of members at this higher developmental position who are not invested in preserving the organisation as-it-is, it will be better fitted to navigate the turbulence of our times, reforming and transforming itself in continuous, self-organising change. And it will also be ready to participate in the renewal of our failing global systems – as, increasingly, all its stakeholders expect it to do – because it will have a greater purpose, a more meaningful role to play in the world, than simply to exist to maintain itself.

How I, as someone with responsibility for the development ground of my organisation, may manage the task of providing an appropriate holding environment for those who are rightfully at the Organisational stage whilst, simultaneously, providing a holding environment which will support those who are moving towards and becoming embedded in the World-Centric stage, is the subject of the Conclusion of this book (for I must assuredly do both). But, before we move on, we can summarise this last chapter with some final additions to our list of rules of the road:

## *The rules of the road.*

1.  The human development journey begins in infancy and, if growth continues, may extend into late adulthood and even until death (some, of course, may say that it extends beyond death).

2.  The path that we, as travellers, follow is one of many distinct stages, each of which represents a clear, qualitative transformation of thinking and being.

3.  The strengths of one stage ultimately become its limitations, a realisation which nudges us to the next stage of our growth.

4.  We progress from one stage to the next by the agency of two fundamental capacities: transcendence and inclusion.

5.  Research has consistently demonstrated that these stages cannot be bypassed without some compromise.

6.  Each stage of the journey offers a new set of challenges (intellectual, social, moral, emotional, psychological and even spiritual challenges) which flow as streams of development through the basic stages of development.

7.  These streams unfold as the stages unfold, by the same agencies of transcendence and inclusion, and also with their own dynamic.

8.  If, in our determination to press onwards, we choose not to confront all the challenges available to us in the streams of development, we will arrive at the next stage of our development with some of our potential unrealised, with an imbalance in our sphere of total capability.

9.  To function as a fully integrated Self, therefore, we must recognise our development gaps and then seek out those stream-specific learning experiences which will enable us to attend to them.

10. How we embrace these learning experiences will be influenced, in some measure, by our own personality.

11. The more we understand our personality, the more we understand the range of behavioural choices available to us.

12. Knowing when and how to act 'in character' and when and how to act 'out of character' – whilst still being authentic – equips us to be more effective in a wider and wider range of situations.

13. In order to move forward on our development pathway, however, we must be willing to change; and, in order to change, we must be willing to give up a part of ourselves which, naturally, evokes fear in us, and calls for courage.

14. Happily we are not travelling alone: guides for the journey are available whenever a daunting challenge arises.

15. Masterful guides are those who can create meaningful contact with us, who can read us, who can lead us to a new viewpoint, who can be in the struggle with us, who can effect transformational change in us, and who can also learn from us.

16. If we are willing to be vulnerable, watchful and receptive, we will find the help we need.

17. Each stage of development requires its own culturing context which 'holds' us as we become embedded in it, then 'lets go' of us as we emerge from it (permitting us to explore safely to the edge of our present limits), and then 'remains in place' (enabling us to integrate all our stream-specific learning experiences into our sense of Self) as we move on to our next state of equilibrium.

18. During our working lives, our organisation is our primary development context (because this is where we spend most of our waking hours).

19. If, as adults, we discover that our existing holding environment is not meeting our development needs, it is our responsibility to try to secure an alternative venue for our growth.

20. Finally, we must ensure that we provide an appropriate venue for growth for all those who depend on *us* in order to progress, and we must strive to serve them also as the same masterful guides whom we seek for ourselves.

# Conclusion

*I. Keeping the forest.*

n Chapter Five, we explored the different holding environments which must be in place for us as we make our way on our personal learning journey. We also reflected upon the responsibilities we have to provide appropriate holding environments for those who depend on *us* in order to progress. Now in the Conclusion, we focus specifically on the development ground of the organisation as the primary container for growth in adulthood, and on what may be required of those whose responsibility it is to create and sustain it, on behalf of those who work within it.

In any organisation there will be people at different stages of their development. The majority may well have achieved the Organisational stage but younger members (in their late adolescence or early twenties) and, indeed, some chronologically aged mature adults may still be at, or emerging from, the Relational stage. Some members, meanwhile, may have achieved the World-Centric stage.

At the same time, given that each stream of development unfolds with its own dynamic and that our passage along them is not necessarily uniform, there will, in any organisation, be people with different stream-related challenges to attend to, as well.

Those who 'take care' of organisations need to ensure, therefore, that they provide appropriate culturing contexts for everyone. The metaphor of the forest illustrates that the entity of the organisation is the ground of all the development which occurs within it – the total of all the holding environments available, the venue for all challenges met, challenges denied, challenges failed and challenges yet to come.

## II. *The business case for keeping the forest.*

he business case for investing resources in 'keep-ing the forest' rests on a proposition of *inter-dependence* and *interdevelopment*, which assumes that if development theory holds true for individ-uals, then it must also hold true for organisations, since they are, essentially, groups of such individuals operating together over a period of time within the same culture. By impli-cation, the mean stage of development that the members of an organisation have reached defines the stage of development that the organisation has reached.

This proposition is not a new one – a number of theorists have offered models for the development of organisations which are analogous to the models which have been offered for the develop-ment of organisms. Two well-known examples are:

1. The Viable Systems model of the management cyberneti-cian, Stafford Beer, which describes how a viable organisation (i.e. a system which intends to survive) can learn, adapt and evolve second-by-second to meet the demands of its changing internal and external environments. It is derived from the "admirable and survival-worthy" control systems of human neurophysiology.[1]

2. A model proposed by the leadership scholar, William Tor-bert, which consists of a set of leadership transformations (or leadership styles, each of which represents a more sophisticated position than the previous one) and a corresponding set of organi-sation development stages (which extend from the fantasies of an organisation's creators at its inception, to maturity).[2] Torbert – who was influenced by, amongst others, the now-familiar names of Jean Piaget, Jane Loevinger and Robert Kegan but notably, too, by the life-stage theorist Erik Erikson – observes, with his co-writer, David Rooke, that "those who do undertake a voyage of personal understanding can transform not just their own capa-bilities but also those of their companies".[3]

Torbert reminds us that there is a long history of scholarly debate about the validity of such comparisons[4] and, as the author of this book, I do not propose to join that argument. My position is, simply, that most organisations, whilst made up of people, are clearly *intentionally designed constructs*, and so I would not necessarily expect them to develop in the same way as living organisms. But I do note that once an organisation has formed, it does exhibit some fundamental characteristics of living organisms, particularly human organisms, by striving for, for example, greater complexity, greater integration and greater differentiation in its own project of evolution, and so I believe we can identify a sequence of developmental stages which may be applied to it. And, given the pivotal role of the organisation's senior leaders in shaping it, I also believe (with Torbert and many others) that the mean stage of development that they, *in particular*, have reached will have a defining influence on the stage of development that the whole organisation has reached. (In that ancient story of every human society, the Hero, having reinvented himself in his battles with the giants and dragons that confronted him on his long journey into unknown places, returns to his familiar world and, in his changed state, brings about the collective renewal of the whole community.[5])

So, if an organisation is dominated by people who are lodged at the Imperial stage in one or more of the streams of development, the development environment which prevails will foster imperial-stage behaviour throughout the organisation. A reminder: the Imperial stage is the stage of pre-adolescence at which we are invested in our own needs, interests and wishes. Whilst few adults are 'held' there in terms of their overall development, it is not unusual to find the markings of this stage – in individuals, for example, who struggle to relate to, adapt to, or function with other people effectively; or whose definition of a 'right' act is one which serves their own purposes; or who have difficulty with regulating their emotional responses; or who identify their welfare with that of their reference group, i.e. their own team or their own organisational unit, and whose actions are always in service of securing that particular group's approval. This imperial-stage behaviour will translate into an organisation which exhibits imperial characteristics *itself*. It will be focused on its own needs, interests and wishes. It will be 'clubby' and exclusive. Internal relationships may appear to be strong but, in reality, they will be fragile and fickle. It will like to play by its own rules, and it will not be overly concerned about developments in the wider environment. And we can all envisage the havoc that such an organisation could wreak if it were of a significant size and operating in the global economic system.

If, however, the organisation is dominated by people at the Relational stage (the stage of adolescence at which we are invested in our interpersonal relationships), the prevailing holding environment will foster relational-stage behaviour which will translate into an organisation which *is* relational – focused on business relationships between managers and staff, and between departments and other departments, and between the organisation and the community. This focus, if it is not balanced by a corresponding pragmatism more associated with the Organisational stage, may be achieved at the expense of its commercial survival.

But if, as is most likely, the organisation is dominated by people at the Organisational stage (who joined it because it supports them in their primary ideology, and because it also provides them with a venue in which they can be the autonomous selves they have become), the prevailing holding environment will foster organisational-stage behaviour which will translate into an enterprise which *is* organisational. It will be well-structured and performance-driven. Members will rally around the corporate vision and their own tasks and targets which will have been defined for the purpose of beating or defeating the competition. "People are important" – but not at the expense of the enterprise attaining its business goals or of it maintaining its belief-system and working

principles. Investments will be made in external relationships —
with other organisations and the community — but only to secure
competitive advantage.

In the unlikely event that the organisation is dominated by
people at the World-Centric stage (which, in Western cultures,
only ten per cent of the adult population seem to achieve), the
prevailing holding environment will foster world-centric-stage
behaviour which will translate into an organisation which *is*
world-centric. It will have a bigger purpose than, simply, to maintain itself. It will seek, co-ordinate and utilise the wisdom of
all its members to challenge, stretch and advance its systems of
beliefs and working principles. And it will operate in a way which
attends to the needs of every stakeholder, and which respects and
enhances the opportunities of our interrelated and interdependent world.

The following tables of descriptors will help you identify which
stage of development your own organisation has reached.

# ORGANISATIONAL STAGE

| | |
|---|---|
| *Recruitment and selection* | ❖ Recruitment and selection processes are focused on hiring people who will 'fit in' and who can make a contribution *now*. |
| *Learning* | ❖ Learning is an individual activity and is applied to outdo the competition (which may include other colleagues). |
| *Performance appraisal and reward* | ❖ Remuneration, recognition awards and bonus payments are based on individual achievements, and are allocated individually.<br>❖ Executive pay is out-of-line in comparison to the pay-scales which are applied to the rest of the organisation.<br>❖ Executive bonuses are orientated towards reward for short-term gain rather than long-term share options which require long-term growth for a pay-out.<br>❖ 'Golden parachutes' facilitate the departure of failed leaders even if they created significant losses for the organisation. |
| *Decision-making* | ❖ 'Individual' rather than 'joint' or 'group' decision-making is the norm. |
| *Team-work* | ❖ Team-building activities are regarded as non-essential 'day off' exercises, and the 'team spirit' which is engendered is not sustained 'back in the real world'. |
| *How senior leadership is exercised* | ❖ The 'Executive Suite' is a politically charged, low-trust environment. |
| *External focus* | ❖ Winning, at both the individual and the corporate level, is paramount, with little concern for the impact that this 'winning' has either within or without the organisation. |
| *How people may speak about the organisation* | ❖ "A good place to begin my career."<br>❖ "I can develop here as a professional."<br>❖ "Lots of promotional opportunities."<br>❖ "Good pay and benefits."<br>❖ "Well structured and organised."<br>❖ "It's all about beating the competition."<br>❖ "I am proud of what my organisation is and what it does."<br>❖ "Focused on shareholder value."<br>❖ "Inward-looking, sure of itself, complacent."<br>❖ "A poor neighbour."<br>❖ "Is this where I want to spend the rest of my working life?" |

## CONDITIONS LIKELY TO PREVAIL IN ORGANISATIONS IN THE PROCESS OF TRANSITION FROM THE ORGANISATIONAL TO THE WORLD-CENTRIC STAGE

| | |
|---|---|
| Recruitment and selection | ❖ Recruitment and selection processes are focused on hiring people who will provide some challenge to the system, and who will be able to make a contribution in the future. |
| Learning | ❖ Learning (which may be an individual or group activity) is offered to help participants support the wider organisation. |
| Performance appraisal and reward | ❖ Remuneration, recognition awards and bonus payments are based on individual and team achievements, and are allocated, as appropriate, to individuals and/or teams.<br>❖ Attention is paid to how the 'outside world' may view executive pay rates and bonus schemes as they are being formulated.<br>❖ Failed leaders are dismissed. |
| Decision-making | ❖ Joint problem-solving is the norm. |
| Team-work | ❖ Team members work well together.<br>❖ Whilst there may be rivalry between teams, there is a clear sense of responsibility for 'cross-asset' or 'cross-functional' working, in service of the wider organisation. |
| How senior leadership is exercised | ❖ The 'Executive Team' replaces the 'Executive Suite'.<br>❖ Each member of the executive team embraces an enterprise-wide (rather than an asset-only or function-only) mindset. |
| External focus | ❖ Competition is externally focused.<br>❖ There is an awareness of, and a willingness to avoid or mitigate, the adverse effects of the organisation's activities on its neighbours. |
| How people may speak about the organisation | ❖ "A place to develop both personally and professionally."<br>❖ "I am part of a good team."<br>❖ "I make a difference to the organisation."<br>❖ "Shareholder value is not the only thing that matters."<br>❖ "I was welcomed when I visited."<br>❖ "The organisation responds to feedback."<br>❖ "A good neighbour."<br>❖ "I don't feel fulfilled here." |

## CONDITIONS LIKELY TO PREVAIL IN
## ORGANISATIONS CENTRED AT THE
# WORLD-CENTRIC STAGE

| | |
|---|---|
| *Recruitment and selection* | ❖ Recruitment and selection processes are focused on hiring people who will 'bring the outside in'. |
| *Learning* | ❖ The whole organisation is in a learning relationship with all its stakeholders. |
| *Performance appraisal and reward* | ❖ Remuneration, recognition awards and bonus payments are based on the contribution individuals and teams make to the organisation *and* to the wider community.<br>❖ Executive pay is determined by the organisation's stakeholders.<br>❖ Failed leaders leave of their own volition. |
| *Decision-making* | ❖ All the organisation's stakeholders have a voice in, and influence on, its decision-making processes. |
| *Team-work* | ❖ All members can work with all other members of the organisation – 'the team' is the whole organisation. |
| *How senior leadership is exercised* | ❖ The leadership cadre regard the organisation not as a means to an end but as an integral part of the larger system in which it operates.<br>❖ Part of the organisation's success is attributed to its understanding of the full context within which it exists. |
| *External focus* | ❖ Members are regularly involved in projects which reach beyond the boundaries of the organisation, or of its normal business remit.<br>❖ 'Social responsibility' is more than a set of objectives: it is the core of the organisation's ethos and working practices. |
| *How people may speak about the organisation* | ❖ "I am proud of my organisation's purpose."<br>❖ "A place where I am fulfilled"<br>❖ "The pay and benefits meet my needs."<br>❖ "Change-orientated and innovative."<br>❖ "Committed to making a difference in the world."<br>❖ "An excellent neighbour." |

### III. Embracing the leadership paradox.

wo important principles arise from the proposition of interdependence and interdevelopment described above, which those charged with 'taking care' of their organisation must apply:

- *Principle 1:* To create environments which support the growth of individuals at whatever stage they may be at now, with whatever stream-related challenges they have yet to address.
- *Principle 2:* To create the development ground for moving the whole organisation towards a higher stage of maturity and capability.

The application of these principles, therefore, requires the capacity to embrace a particular leadership paradox: to 'hold' those who are properly (i.e. rightfully) embedded at one of the earlier stages of the human development journey (typically the Organisational stage) whilst, at the same time, nurturing the whole organisation towards the World-Centric stage. (This is a paradox which will be all the more demanding, of course, for those 'keepers' who have yet to make their own transition to the World-Centric stage for they will need to develop as fellow travellers, growing in tandem with their organisation.) To help you in this endeavour, I offer, as suggestions, the following lists of leadership and system-management activities.

| | |
|---|---|
| *How you are* | *Respect the behaviour of those at the Organisational stage.* Young adults at the Organisational stage are very invested in the exercises of self-discipline, personal achievement, pride in themselves and ambition. This behaviour may be irritating to the more mature onlooker but it supports the individuals concerned in the important task of affirming and confirming their newly found autonomy. Be tolerant of this behaviour. |
| *Purpose and vision* | *Generate and articulate a purpose and a vision for the organisation which inspire people to give of their best.* At the Organisational stage, people are embedded in their organisation – they are fused with it, and committed to it because its success and their success are inextricably linked. Define, and clearly communicate to them, a purpose and a vision for the enterprise which offer real competitive advantage, so that they can align themselves with them and be motivated to perform well. |
| *Identity* | *Build a strong sense of identity through a corporate brand which characterises the organisation and sets it apart from similar organisations or competitors.* At the Organisational stage, people are proud of their organisation for what it is and what it does. A strong brand serves the same purpose as a flag or a team mascot – people have an emotional attachment to it and rally around it. Design your organisation's brand so that members can own their relationship to it, and represent it in the wider world. |
| *Values* | *Formulate, and engage people in, a set of values which stretch the definition of what is important to include a commitment to them as individuals.* At the Organisational stage, individuals seek a working environment which offers a venue in which they can be the autonomous selves they have become. Provide them with the opportunities they need to demonstrate their worth and contribution. |

| | |
|---|---|
| *Culture* | *Create a culture which fosters ideas and innovation in order to maintain the organisation's competitive position.* At the Organisational stage, people are ambitious for their organisation as well as for themselves. Nurture this ambition – for it will have obvious bottom-line benefits. Many tools, methods and approaches are available for fostering creativity which may be of help to those who are currently invested in the organisation as-it-is (see, for example, the work of Edward de Bono, Clayton M. Christensen and William C. Miller). |
| *Strategies and objectives* | *Define clear strategies and objectives, and monitor performance against them.* At the Organisational stage, people need to be able to make a contribution which can be appraised according to external measures. Ensure they have tasks and targets which are stretching but achievable, which are measurable (using quantitative gauges) and which are also understood. Review their performance against these measures regularly to enable them to 'stay on track'. |
| *Recognition and reward* | *Construct mechanisms which reward, primarily, the success of individuals.* Effective teamwork may be important for an organisation's overall success but people at the Organisational stage seek recognition for their *individual* achievements. Devise recognition and reward schemes, therefore, which provide proper acknowledgement of such achievements whilst also encouraging synergistic working practices (which are now nothing less than essential in new organisational arrangements such as matrix and networked structures) *as an individual attribute.* |
| *Development processes* | *Enable individuals to develop their skills and capabilities so that they can compete in the internal (and external) marketplace.* People at the Organisational stage have, through the course of their formal education and/or their vocational training, identified a specific route for making a contribution. Support them in their efforts to progress in their chosen discipline or line of work. |

(*continued overleaf*)

*Helping people find Merlin*

*Provide people at the Organisational stage with access to Merlin in a structured way.* From Chapter Four, we know that this work requires you to:

1. Make contact with them as one individual (you) with another (him/her).
2. Provide feedback to help them identify which challenges they have met and which challenges they have yet to address in the various streams of development associated with the Organisational stage.
3. Help them to make meaning of their experiences in an organisational-stage context.
4. Help them to find solutions *as autonomous people* to the challenges they still face at the Organisational stage.
5. Effect transformational change in them by, at the right time, indicating to them that they are ready to move on from their autonomous way of working and make the transition to the World-Centric stage, whilst still being available to them to help them integrate their achievements of the Organisational stage into their new sense of Self.
6. Identify ways to learn from them – notwithstanding the fact that you may have progressed further than they have along the human development road.

At first reading, much of the above seems to represent the standard fare of any management textbook. This should not surprise us. As we noted in Chapter Five, the business case for holding people at the Organisational stage has, in previous decades at least, been very strong, and the textbooks have, of course, captured the best practice which has emerged from those times. But this best practice has not evolved with conscious attention to development theory. In order to be effective, therefore, the interventions described above must be designed with that theory in mind – 'standard' approaches, in other words, may need modification.

But what, in addition, must the 'keepers' of an organisational system do to create the right culturing context which will support members as they make their transition to the World-Centric stage, and as they seek to function there as a fully integrated Self?

LEADERSHIP AND SYSTEM-MANAGEMENT ACTIVITIES
WHICH WILL SUPPORT THE MOVEMENT OF PEOPLE TOWARDS
THE WORLD-CENTRIC STAGE AND
ENABLE THEM TO CONSOLIDATE THEIR POSITION THERE

*How you
are*

*Be World-Centric yourself!* When the 'keepers' of an organisation are maintaining a holding environment which supports the development of members who are at the Organisational stage, there are many things they must do (such as those activities listed above). When they are maintaining a holding environment which supports the progression of members towards the World-Centric stage and which enables them to consolidate their position there, their focus must be on 'being' as much as it is on 'doing'. In particular, this means exercising their leadership in a way which is consistent with the achievements of the World-Centric stage. So, refer to the list of the defining characteristics of world-centric leadership in Chapter One (and repeated in Chapter Five); measure yourself against them; and take whatever action is necessary to attend to any shortfalls. Remember: role-modelling world-centric behaviour does not simply 'show the way' to others; importantly, it also gives them permission to be different people from who they were when they were at the Organisational stage.

NB: If you believe that you have attained the World-Centric stage of your personal development journey, and if you concluded that you have met Abraham Maslow's conditions for 'readiness' in the self-inquiry exercise you completed as you read Chapter Four, ask yourself now: Have I made the transition yet to the state of 'self-actualisation'? If the answer to this question is 'No', there is more personal work for you to do before you can live at the World-Centric stage with all the potential which is available to you, because the fullest expression of the World-Centric stage is the state of 'self-actualisation'.

(*continued overleaf*)

| | |
|---|---|
| *Purpose and vision* | *Generate and articulate a purpose and vision for the organisation which propose a greater possibility than simply maintaining itself.* People who are at the World-Centric stage want to be part of an organisation which is bigger than itself – something which is more than just a 'top-quartile performer'. They can envisage the role their organisation could play in the world, so involve them in creating a purpose and a vision for the enterprise which capture that possibility. |
| *Identity* | *Build a strong sense of identity through a corporate brand which instils pride in members because it represents the organisation's broad perspective and commitments.* What people are proud of with respect to their organisation does not change as they progress to the World-Centric stage; it expands. Develop your organisation's brand to represent more to them and the wider community than just competitive advantage. |
| *Values* | *Involve people in formulating a set of values which stretch the definition of what is important to include forging relationships of mutual respect and influence.* People at the World-Centric stage have renounced the socio-centric stance in which they were previously invested and seek working arrangements of real connection – with colleagues, suppliers, customers, the community, and so on. Involve them in formulating a set of values which incorporate this need. |
| *Culture* | *Create a culture which facilitates group thinking to unleash the diversity that is available.* Participatory thinking is the medium of insight for people at the World-Centric stage: those involved rise above themselves and their opinions, diversity flourishes, and the group mind is engaged. Many well-proven methods are available to facilitate this inclusive, generative activity such as Future Search, Appreciative Inquiry, The World Café, Open Space, Dialogue and The Conference Model. Employ them to solve those 'wicked problems' and 'social messes' which present so frequently today in our living and working as members of an interrelated and interdependent global community. |

| | |
|---|---|
| *Strategies and objectives* | *Create clear strategies and objectives which ensure that the promise of the organisation's purpose and vision can be realised.* Social responsibility programmes are often undertaken as peripheral, 'must-do' activities for reputation purposes only. People at the World-Centric stage, however, know that being 'socially responsible' is, simply, 'being responsible', and that, when an organisation expands its boundaries to 'bring the outside in', the 'outside' becomes a greater and greater resource for it. Create strategies and objectives which embrace 'the outside' as an 'opportunity' both for the organisation and the wider world, instead of limiting it as an 'inconvenience' or a 'constraint'. |
| *Recognition and reward* | *Construct mechanisms which balance individual success with teamwork and with the contribution made to the organisation's purpose and vision.* People at the World-Centric stage are more concerned with self-fulfilment than with achievement. Devise recognition and reward schemes, therefore, which encourage and support the attainment of this goal (note that such schemes should involve qualitative as well as quantitative measures). |
| *Development processes* | *Search the broader environment for development opportunities which expose individuals to different places and experiences, and so create valuable learning for the whole organisation.* Regression is possible! People do need to be 'held' at the World-Centric stage in order to become embedded in it. The wider environment can be their learning laboratory if you employ it effectively. Then select future leaders for the organisation from the pool who have been exposed to these external development opportunities – those whom you can distinguish not by what they *do* (as measured by competency models) but by who they *are*. Remember: without process, many things do not happen in organisations; with process, you can bring intentions into being. |

*(continued overleaf)*

*Helping people find Merlin*

*Connect people to people at the World-Centric stage.* From Chapter Four, we know that this work requires you to:

1. Facilitate contact between you and them, and between them and each other, in interdependent relationships.

2. Provide feedback to help them identify which challenges they have met and which challenges they have yet to address in the various streams of development associated with the World-Centric stage.

3. Help them to make meaning of their experiences in a world-centric-stage context.

4. Help them to find solutions *as people who belong to a community of being* to the challenges they still face at the World-Centric stage.

5. Effect transformational change in them by helping them to incorporate all their achievements in the different streams of development, and so consolidate their position at the World-Centric stage, so that 'self-actualisation' becomes a possibility.

6. Identify ways to learn from them as fellow travellers on the human development road.

## IV. *The final call to action.*

f we do not want to number ourselves amongst those who "do not amount to much"[6], if we do not want to "sleep before evening"[7], we must commit to move forward on our personal learning journey:

"I am a part of all that I have met;
Yet all experience is an arch wherethro'
Gleams that untravell'd world, whose margin fades
For ever and for ever when I move.
How dull it is to pause, to make an end,
To rust unburnish'd, not to shine in use!
As tho' to breathe were life."[8]

What does this mean? It means mustering the courage to take the difficult, truly developmental path at the next fork we encounter on the human development road. It means working at the intersection of our Self with our organisation with a spirit of adventure and imagination, creating and making those wise choices which will enable us to overcome the many and various challenges that confront us, and seeking out those heroic teachers who can show us the way.

When, however, we assume a position of leadership in an organisation, we have a special developmental responsibility – not just to ourselves but to those whom we lead, and to the enterprise we have been entrusted to steward. We are charged with providing culturing contexts – places where magic can happen – which will enable people and the organisation to grow and contribute to their fullest potential, to be a world-centric force for good in this fragmented and individualistic yet also interrelated and interdependent world in which we all now live and work. Finding Merlin *and* being Merlin, is, therefore, both an opportunity for us and an obligation.

What is my life's work? What kind of organisation am I constructing? What legacy will I leave? And who do I need to *be* in order that these possibilities may be realised? These are important questions that all of us in leadership positions should ask of ourselves at mid-life; and global events of recent years, of course, lend them a new imperative. To all who read this book, therefore, I wish you well as you ride onwards on your own pathway of growth – however far and wherever it takes you.

# Notes

NOTES TO THE INTRODUCTION

1  See Chapter One of *The Unending Mystery, A Journey Through Labyrinths and Mazes* by David Willis McCullough (New York: Anchor Books, 2005).

2  To learn more about labyrinths and mazes, see ibid.

3  The first *Story of the Grail* was written by the French romancer, Chrétien de Troyes, in the 1180s, but it was never completed. There is nothing so compelling as an unfinished story and, for centuries, it has intrigued both writers (who created their own continuations) and readers alike.

4  The pre-eminent developmental psychologist, Robert Kegan, writes: "...the activity of being a person is the activity of meaning-making." See *The Evolving Self* (Cambridge, Massachusetts: Harvard University Press, 1982), p 11. © 1982 by the President and Fellows of Harvard College. Reprinted by permission of the publisher.

5  See *The Journey as a Metaphor* in *Myth and Metaphor, Selected Essays 1974–1988* by Northrop Frye, edited by Robert D. Denham (Charlottesville: University of Virginia Press, 2000), p 221. © 1990 by the Rector and Visitors of the University of Virginia.

6  The literary critic, Northrop Frye, provides us with this useful distinction: the 'way' is the road, path or direction taken; when the way enters the life of the individual we have the form of the journey we call the 'quest' ("where a hero goes out to accomplish something, kill a dragon, deliver a heroine from a giant, help destroy a hostile city, or what not"). Ibid, p 213.

7  See *A Brief History of Everything* by Ken Wilber (Dublin: Gateway Books, an imprint of Gill and Macmillan, 2001).

8  In Wolfram von Eschenbach's celebrated Middle High German text, *Parzival* (which is a recreation and continuation of Chrétien de Troye's unfinished *Story of the Grail*, and which is summarised in Chapter One of this book), the hero is "trâclîche wîs", 'slowly wise'. See *Wolfram's Parzival* by Otto Springer in *Arthurian Literature in the Middle Ages: A Collaborative History*, edited by Roger Sherman Loomis (Oxford: Oxford University Press, 2001), p 226.

9  See *The Great Transformation: The World in the Time of Buddha, Socrates, Confucius and Jeremiah* by Karen Armstrong (London: Atlantic Books, 2007) pp xiv and xvi.

10  See *Career Dynamics: Matching Individual and Organizational Needs* by Edgar Schein (Reading, Mass.: Addison-Wesley Publishing Company, 1978).

11 The chivalric hero, Perceval, in the first accounts and the spiritually trium-
    phant Galahad in the later versions.

12 See *The Road Less Traveled: A New Psychology of Love, Traditional Values and
    Spiritual Growth* by M. Scott Peck (New York: Touchstone, 2003), p 17. The
    term 'legitimate suffering' was originally proposed by the psychologist, Carl
    Gustav Jung (1973).

13 See *Deep Change: Discovering the Leader Within* by Robert Quinn (San Fran-
    cisco, California: Jossey-Bass, 1996), p 3. Reprinted with permission from
    John Wiley and Sons, Inc.

14 See *The Hero with a Thousand Faces* by Joseph Campbell (London: Fontana
    Press, 1993).

15 See 'Teaching Smart People How To Learn' by Chris Argyris, *Harvard Busi-
    ness Review*, May–June 1991, Reprint 91301, p 10.

16 See *Organising Genius: The Secret of Creative Collaboration* by Warren Bennis
    and Patricia Ward Biederman (Cambridge, Mass.: Perseus Books, 1997), p 2.

17 Ibid, pp 3 and 198.

18 See *Ulysses* by Alfred, Lord Tennyson.

19 See the Conclusion of *The Renaissance* by Walter Pater.

NOTES TO CHAPTER ONE: THE PATH THROUGH THE FOREST

1 *The Holy Grail* by Richard Barber (London: Penguin Books, 2004), repro-
    duced by permission of Penguin Books Ltd. Adapted and reprinted by
    permission of the publisher from *The Holy Grail: Imagination and Belief*
    (Cambridge, Mass.: Harvard University Press) in the USA, © 2004 by Rich-
    ard Barber.

2 See the Introduction to this book.

3 The motif of the Quest was employed extensively in the literature of the
    Middle Ages – a time when allegorical ways of writing which focused on
    the internal world (the proper conduct of life and the final destination of the
    soul) were dominant. See *Allegory* by John MacQueen (London and New
    York: Methuen, 1970).

4 Details provided in this chapter of the date, the number of lines and chap-
    ters, and the number of surviving manuscripts of Wolfram von Eschenbach's
    *Parzival* are drawn from *Wolfram's Parzival* by Otto Springer, op cit, pp 220,
    247 and 249.

5 In the course of his adventures, Parzival becomes "trâclîche wîs" or 'slowly
    wise' – the singularly pregnant phrase Wolfram von Eschenbach uses to
    characterise his hero's gradual inner growth. Ibid, p 226.

6 See *The Great Chain of Being* by Arthur O. Lovejoy (New York and London:
    Transaction Publishers, 2009; originally published in 1936 by Harvard Uni-
    versity Press), for a history of this idea.

7   Adapted from *A Brief History of Everything* by Ken Wilber, who was influenced by, amongst many others, the philosopher of science, Erwin Laszlo – pp 31–33.

8   Ibid, p 36.

9   Summarised from the translation by A.T. Hatto (London: Penguin Books, 1980).

10  See Loomis, p 246.

11  This regressive process of synapse elimination proceeds as an orderly sequence of 'sensitive periods', which may be defined as brief windows of vulnerability, of need, and also of opportunity. Provided new stimuli are presented to children in a way which is attuned to their developmental stage, organised development will occur. But, as many studies have demonstrated, toxins (including chronic stress), poor nutrition, neglect and failure of environmental stimulation may lead to permanent deficits in mental functioning.

12  This associational process was defined by the psychologist, Donald Hebb, in 1949: "...any two cells or systems of cells that are repeatedly active at the same time will tend to become 'associated', so that activity in one facilitates activity in the other". The simple axiom, 'neurons that fire together wire together', describes Hebb's law. See *The Developing Mind* by Daniel J. Siegel (New York: The Guilford Press, 1999), p 26.

13  See 'A Conception of Early Adolescence' by Jerome Kagan in *Twelve to Sixteen: Early Adolescence*, edited by Jerome Kagan and Robert Coles (New York: W.W. Norton and Company Inc, 1972), p 91.

14  To learn more about the development of the brain and the mind, see Siegel, op cit.

15  See, for example, 'Neurogenesis in Adult Mammals: Some Progress and Problems', by Elizabeth Gould and Charles G. Gross in *The Journal of Neuroscience*, 1 February 2002, and 'Mapping Changes in the Human Cortex Throughout the Span of Life' by Elizabeth R. Sowell, Paul M. Thompson and Arthur W. Toga in *The Neuroscientist*, Volume 10, Number 4, 2004.

16  *The Psychology of Aging* by Ian Stuart-Hamilton (London and Philadelphia: Jessica Kingsley Publishers, 2006) p 97. Reproduced with kind permission of Jessica Kingsley Publishers.

17  *The Human Mind* by Robert Winston (London: Bantam Press, 2004), p 77. Used by permission of the Random House Group Ltd.

18  *The Perennial Philosophy* by Aldous Huxley (New York: Harper Perennial Modern Classics, 2009; first published in 1945), p vii. Copyright 1944, 1945 by Aldous Huxley. Copyright renewed 1973, 1974 by Laura A. Huxley. Reprinted by permission of HarperCollins Publishers.

19  Kegan, op cit, p 30.

20 Ibid.

21 Ibid, pp 129–30.

22 Joseph Chiltern Pearce in *The Magical Child* (New York: Plume, a division of Penguin Books, 1992) describes very clearly how the primary carer ("the cornerstone of meaning", p 89) provides the older infant and child with a conceptual channel for interacting with and responding to the world; and how the child, whilst exploring the world on his or her own, needs to be able to return immediately to the safety and security that the carer represents whenever necessary, in order to be able to accommodate new experiences and so build the "muscular-mindedness" which will lead eventually to autonomy (p 32).

23 Kegan, op cit, p 136.

24 Ibid, pp 26–27.

25 Ibid, p 139.

26 Ibid.

27 See *Developmental Social Psychology, From Infancy to Old Age* by Kevin Durkin (Malden, Massachusetts: Blackwell Publishing, 2003), p 143.

28 Kegan, op cit, p 167, who reproduced the list of clubhouse rules from *The New Yorker* (18 September 1954), p 31. Copyright © 1954 Condé Nast. All rights reserved. Originally published in *The New Yorker*. Reprinted by permission.

29 Kegan, op cit, p 100.

30 Ibid, p 205.

31 Ibid, p 211.

32 Ibid, p 96.

33 Ibid, p 222.

34 Durkin, op cit, p 548.

35 Recruitment efforts in organisations of all types (commercial firms, public services, charities, the military, religious organisations, political parties, trade unions, pressure groups and so on) which are focused on selecting young people at the Organisational stage of their development are seeking not just those who are, typically, educationally ready to enter the workplace but those who are also prepared to commit with intensity to an ideology or a system of beliefs.

36 See Kegan, op cit, p 101.

37 Ibid, pp 242–47.

38 Wilber, op cit, p 170.

39 See 'The Healing Power of Systems Change in a Fragile World' by Louise Diamond, *Practising Social Change* (online journal of the NTL Institute for Applied Behavioural Science), Edition 01, p 4. www.ntl.org.

40 Wilber, op cit, p 143.

41 Peck, op cit, p 192–93.

42 Ibid, p 96.

43 I refer readers who are interested in learning more about the stage of Self-Transcendence to the work of Ken Wilber.

44 See, for example, 'The Tale of the Sangrail' in *Le Morte Darthur* by Sir Thomas Malory.

## NOTES TO CHAPTER TWO: GIANTS AND DRAGONS

1 *The Winchester Manuscript of Le Morte Darthur*, edited and abridged by Helen Cooper (Oxford: Oxford University Press, 1998), p 211. The traditional title of Malory's great work is supplied in a colophon at the end of the text by his first printer, William Caxton, without regard to the grammatical rules of the French language. Quoted extract reproduced by permission of Oxford University Press.

2 See the Introduction to this book.

3 Peter Reason, *Participation in Human Inquiry* (London: Sage Publications, 1994), p 192, citing Herb Shepard ('Rule VIII: Capture the moment', 1975), a pioneering thinker in the Organisation Development movement.

4 More than twenty streams of development have been identified so far by the theorists. In this book I describe the six that I regard as the most relevant to people in their organisational lives: the Intellectual, Social, Moral, Emotional, Psychological and Spiritual streams.

5 See *The Psychology of the Child* by Jean Piaget and Bärbel Inhelder (New York: Basic Books, 2000; first published in 1969) to learn more about Piaget's theory. See p 98 specifically to learn about this particular conservation task.

6 Kegan, op cit, p 32.

7 Kagan, 'A Conception of Early Adolescence', pp 92–93.

8 Wilber, op cit, p 169.

9 See *Introductory Psychology* by Tony Malim and Anne Birch (Basingstoke: Macmillan Press, 1998), pp 459–67, for a comprehensive account of Piaget's theory of cognitive development and criticisms thereof.

10 See *Ego Development* by Jane Loevinger (San Francisco: Jossey-Bass Publishers, 1976), Chapter Two.

11 See 'A Neo-Piagetian Perspective on Adult Cognitive Development' by Gisela Labouvie-Vief in *Intellectual Development*, edited by Robert J. Sternberg and Cynthia A. Berg (Cambridge: Cambridge University Press, 1992), pp 197–223.

12 See *On Dialogue* by David Bohm (London and New York: Routledge Classics, 2004).

13 It is important to distinguish here between *social influence*, which involves complex processes of interpersonal negotiations, and *compliance*, which is a

behavioural acknowledgement of superior forces, and need not necessarily imply any underlying change or development in the individual. See Durkin, op cit, p 12.

14 Siegel, op cit, p 2.

15 See Durkin, op cit.

16 Ibid, Chapter Two.

17 There is some theoretical dispute about the origins of attachment and exactly how it contributes to subsequent development. Research has demonstrated, though, that different orientations towards child-rearing are associated with differences in sociability and social behaviour, and there is extensive evidence that *secure attachment* is associated with positive social outcomes. See Durkin, op cit, p 119.

18 Siegel, op cit, p 67.

19 See Durkin, op cit, pp 93–94.

20 See *Siblings: Love, Envy and Understanding* by Judy Dunn and Carol Kendrick (London: Grant McIntyre, 1982), p 84.

21 See Durkin, op cit, Chapter Four

22 Pro-social behaviour varies across cultures: in different social environments different expectations, examples and endorsements of pro-social behaviour prevail. Many Western nations, for example, tend to value individualism, with an emphasis on personal responsibility and achievement. Other, collectivist societies, such as the People's Republic of China, stress the obligations of the citizen to her or his community, valuing loyalty, trust and co-operation. These cultural orientations lead to an emphasis on self-reliance in the individualist cultures, and on social conformity in the collectivist cultures. This may, in turn, lead to variations in the degree of pro-social behaviour displayed by the young of these different societies. See Durkin, op cit, p 458.

23 This model of social competence is an *information-processing* account of our behavioural responses to social situations, and illustrates the role that the achievements of the Intellectual stream play in the unfolding of the Social stream: a well-differentiated sense of Self with regard to a clearly represented 'other' plus information-processing skills are necessary for optimal social exchanges. But note that the application of the five steps is assumed to occur rapidly and often at a non-conscious level. As the authors of this model emphasise, other factors such as a self-concept (see the Psychological stream) and emotions (see the Emotional stream) will also play an organising role in our social exchanges – see 'Social Competence in Children' by Kenneth A. Dodge et al in *Monographs of the Society for Research in Child Development*, Serial No 213, Vol 51, No 2. As we noted earlier in this chapter, the streams of development unfold in both a dependent and an independent relationship with each other.

24  See Durkin, op cit, Chapter Fifteen.

25  Ibid, p 652.

26  Ibid, Chapters Eighteen and Nineteen

27  Ibid, p 650–52, citing Komarovsky (1987), Rossi and Rossi (1990), Aizenberg and Treas (1985) and Stroebe and Stroebe (1987).

28  Ibid, p 14.

29  Two long-standing philosophical traditions offering very different moral systems are available to mankind, as the philosopher, A.C. Grayling, explains: "…when one looks at the best that has been thought and said about the good life for human beings, it transpires that there are two large but very different conceptions of what that should be, which have remained consistent in essentials through time. One is a broadly secular attitude rooted in views about human nature and the human condition. The other is a broadly transcendental one that locates the source of moral value outside the human realm…." *What Is Good? The Search for the Best Way to Live* by A.C. Grayling (London: Weidenfeld & Nicolson, an imprint of the Orion Publishing Group, 2004) © 2003 A.C. Grayling, p 1. The moral system described in *Finding Merlin* is not a religion-based code of morality; it is, expressly, a humanistic one.

30  The anthropologist, Christopher Hallpike, describes how our interaction with others is central to the development of our moral understanding. Mankind's range of moral concern has steadily extended from our immediate kin and neighbours to include human beings as a whole, as, over millennia, our social organisations have grown more complex (from hunter-gatherer bands to larger, more permanent agrarian societies, to the emergence of states), with each development offering increasing levels of contact with other societies and, therefore, new social experiences to stimulate moral thinking. Controversially, perhaps, he asserts that the full extent of moral development is not attained by those living in small-scale societies such as isolated tribal or island communities. Other researchers have reached the same conclusion. See *The Evolution of Moral Understanding* by Christopher R. Hallpike (Alton: Prometheus Research Group, 2004).

31  Grayling, op cit, p 1.

32  See, for example, 'The Adolescent as a Philosopher' by Lawrence Kohlberg and Carol Gilligan, in Kagan and Coles, op cit, pp 145–79, for a description of Kohlberg's six moral perspectives.

33  *In a Different Voice: Psychological Theory and Women's Development* by Carol Gilligan (Cambridge Massachusetts: Harvard University Press, 1993), pp xvii–xviii. © 1982, 1993 by Carol Gilligan. Reprinted by permission of Harvard University Press.

34  Summarised, for example, by Durkin, op cit, Chapter Fourteen.

35 Gilligan, op cit, p 73.

36 See *The Development of Social Knowledge: Morality and Convention* by Elliot Turiel (Cambridge: Cambridge University Press, 2003).

37 "Clearly, the human brain is sufficiently different from the brains of other animals to give us reasons for being very cautious about attributing consciousness beyond our species." *The Emotional Brain* by Joseph LeDoux, (London: Phoenix, an imprint of Orion Publishing Group Ltd, 1998), p 301.

38 Different theorists have proposed different lists of basic emotions, but most include some version of fear, anger, disgust and joy. From the nineteenth-century naturalist, Charles Darwin, onwards, they have observed that, notwithstanding cross-cultural variation in the display rules, these emotions are expressed in broadly similar ways, particularly with regard to the movement of facial muscles. These universal expressions of emotion, examples of which Darwin identified in both humans and animals, convinced him and successive researchers that many of our emotions have a long evolutionary history.

39 LeDoux, op cit, p 20.

40 Different emotions are mediated by separate neural systems which have evolved for different reasons, but current research suggests that all emotional feelings and all emotional responses are effects which are likely to be caused by the activity of a common underlying system, as described by LeDoux.

41 Adapted from LeDoux, op cit, p 164.

42 LeDoux, op cit, p 165.

43 *Emotional Intelligence: Why It Can Matter More Than IQ* by Daniel Goleman, (London: Bloomsbury Publishing Plc, 1996), p 5.

44 Aristotle, *The Nicomachean Ethics*.

45 See *Emotional Development: The Organization of Emotional Life in the Early Years* by L. Alan Sroufe (Cambridge: Cambridge University Press, 1997). © Cambridge University Press 1995, reproduced with permission.

46 LeDoux, op cit, p 66.

47 Sroufe, op cit, pp 57–58.

48 LeDoux, op cit, p 302.

49 See Sroufe, op cit, p 40. These more complex emotions may be special human experiences with a much shorter evolutionary history than the basic emotions described earlier.

50 Sroufe notes the seeming paradox of the infant who is effectively dependent – who operates successfully from within the caregiver-infant relationship – and who is also the child who later shows more effective functioning outside this relationship, i.e. is more capable of independent functioning. Ibid, p 151.

51 Ibid, Chapter Eleven.

52 LeDoux, op cit, p 25.

53  Goleman, op cit, pp 177 and 183.

54  Ibid, p 227.

55  See Loevinger, op cit, Chapter Two.

56  As an illustration of the organising role of the ego, the identity of the child at the Impulsive level of the Psychological stream described in this paragraph is clearly integrating all her achievements in the Intellectual, Social, Emotional and Moral streams.

57  Loevinger believed that the *self-aware* position is a period of transition between the preceding *conformist* and the succeeding *conscientious* positions, but noted that this period was transitional only in a theoretical sense because it appears to be a stable level of identity development for many in mature life.

58  "Where the Self-Protective person obeys rules in order to avoid getting into trouble and the Conformist obeys rules because the group sanctions them, the Conscientious person evaluates and chooses the rules for himself." Loevinger, op cit, pp 20–21.

59  As with the *self-aware* position, Loevinger described the *individualistic* position as a period of transition between the previous one and the succeeding one (see note above).

60  "At this level… the conflict, for example, over marriage versus a career for a woman, is likely to be seen as only partly internal. If only society or one's husband were more helpful and accommodating, there need be no conflict. That conflict is part of the human condition is not recognised until the Autonomous Stage." Loevinger, op cit, p 22.

61  With reference to the inclusion here of the capacity to embrace uncertainty and flux, see the authors' note in the description of the Intellectual stream.

62  Maslow was interested in motivation, and proposed a classification of hierarchically organised human needs beginning with the physical needs of air, food and water, followed by four levels of psychological needs – for safety, love, esteem and, finally, self-actualisation. Higher needs, which are as real and integral a part of human nature as the need for air, food and water, are less demanding and can be postponed longer, but the satisfaction of them produces more happiness and leads to greater individual growth.

63  *Motivation and Personality* by Abraham H. Maslow, revised by Robert Frager, James Fadiman, Cynthia McReynolds and Ruth Cox (Upper Saddle River, New Jersey: Pearson Education, Inc., 1987), p 126.

64  Ibid, p 140.

65  Ibid, p xxvi.

66  Ibid, p xxxv.

67  Karen Armstrong, *A History of God* (London: William Heineman, 1999), p 3. Reprinted by permission of the Random House Group Ltd.

68 See *Stages of Faith: The Psychology of Human Development and the Quest for Meaning* by James W. Fowler (New York: HarperOne, 1995). Copyright © 1981 James W. Fowler. Reprinted by permission of HarperCollins Publishers.

69 See *Faith Development and Fowler*, edited by Craig Dykstra and Sharon Parks (Birmingham, Alabama: Religious Education Press, 1986).

70 See Fowler, op cit, p 121.

71 Ibid, pp 133–34.

72 See ibid, pp 135–36, for this description of the Mythic-Literal Stage of Faith.

73 See ibid, pp 152–54, 173–74, for this description of the Synthetic-Conventional Stage of Faith

74 Fowler cites as an example of the activity of demythologising a story recounted to him by the theologian Harvey Cox, who, as a high-school boy, attended a Christmas Eve mass with his girlfriend, a student of anthropology. As the mass climaxed and the congregation was receiving the Eucharist, she whispered to him, "That's just a primitive totemic ritual, you know…. Almost all premodern religious and tribal groups have them. They are ceremonies where worshippers bind themselves together and to the power of the sacred by a cannibalistic act of ingesting the mana of a dead god." And Cox reported that Communion was never the same again for him: "A symbol recognised as a symbol is a broken symbol". Fowler, op cit, pp 180–81.

75 See ibid, pp 180–83, for this description of the Individuative-Reflective Stage of Faith

76 See ibid, pp 186–87, 198–99, for this description of the Conjunctive Level of Faith.

77 Ibid, p 200.

78 Peck, op cit, p 96.

79 Wilber differentiates between *Cosmic* Consciousness, "where all beings are seen in equal light, with no hierarchy at all, no higher or lower, just the great web of life", and the hierarchical organisation of levels of awareness, which he describes as *Kosmic* Consciousness. Wilber, op cit, pp 33–35.

80 Those readers who are interested in learning more about these maps will find them described in chapters twelve and thirteen of Ken Wilber's *A Brief History of Everything*.

81 Wilber, op cit, p 181.

82 Armstrong, op cit, p 4.

83 Wilber, op cit, p 39.

84 See Jill Mann, 'Malory: Knightly Combat in Le Morte D'Arthur', in *Medieval Literature: Chaucer and the Alliterative Tradition*, edited by Boris Ford (London: Penguin Books, 1994), p 333.

NOTES TO CHAPTER THREE: THE KNIGHT ADVENTUROUS

1   *The Winchester Manuscript of Le Morte Darthur*, op cit, pp 321–22.

2   See Malim and Birch, op cit, p 705, citing I.L. Child in *Personality in Culture* in *Handbook of Personality Theory and Research*, edited by E.F. Borgatta and W.W. Lambert (Chicago: Rand McNally, 1968), p 83. The 'factors' referred to here might include cognitive or emotional patterns, structures such as values, beliefs or attitudes, or a self-concept which incorporates one's interpreted experiences, or a mixture of all of them.

3   See *Early Blazon: Heraldic Terminology in the Twelfth and Thirteenth Centuries with Special Reference to Arthurian Heraldry* by Gerard J. Brault (Woodbridge: The Boydell Press, 1997), pp 46–47.

4   See *The Symbolisms of Heraldry* by William Cecil Wade (London: George Redway, 1898), available today as part of the BiblioLife Reproduction Series, for an account of the symbolic meaning of medieval blazon.

5   See the editorial notes of Helen Cooper in the Oxford World Classics edition of *Le Morte Darthur* (Oxford: Oxford University Press, 1998).

6   See the article on 'Heraldry' by Oswald Barron in the eleventh edition of Encyclopædia Britannica, 1911.

7   See Malim and Burch, op cit, p 706.

8   Ibid.

9   See ibid, Part Seven, to learn more about the questions which present when the subject of personality is studied closely.

10  Durkin, op cit, p 70.

11  To learn more about the whole subject of personality, see Part Seven of Malim and Birch, op cit, pp 705–743, and Durkin, op cit, pp 70–1.

12  This description of the Five Factor Model and its development is drawn from 'Updating Norman's "Adequate Taxonomy": Intelligence and Personality Dimensions in Natural Language and in Questionnaires' by Robert R. McCrae and Paul T. Costa Jr in *Journal of Personality and Social Psychology* 49 (1985), pp 710–21, and also from 'An Introduction to the Five Factor Model and its Applications' by Robert R. McCrae and Oliver P. John in *Journal of Personality* 60 (2006; published by John Wiley and Sons Ltd), pp 175–215.

13  One recent study has indicated a maturation effect. Levels of Agreeableness and Conscientiousness were found to increase, typically, with time; Openness showed small declines; and Extraversion and Neuroticism declined with age for women but not men. See 'Development of Personality in Early and Middle Adulthood: Set Like Plaster or Persistent Change' by Sanjay Srivastava, Oliver P. John, Samuel Gosling and Jeff Potter in *Journal of Personality and Social Psychology* 84, No 5 (2003), pp 1041–53. Another study has indicated that people demonstrate unique patterns of personality change at all

stages of their life course as a result of their specific life experiences. See 'Personality Trait Change in Adulthood' by Brent W. Roberts and Daniel Mroczek in *Current Directions in Psychological Science*, Volume 17 (2008), pp 31–35.

14  See McCrae and John, op cit, p 207.

15  Ibid, p 188.

16  This description of the Myers-Briggs Type Instrument and its development is drawn from *Jung: A Very Short Introduction* by Anthony Stevens (Oxford: Oxford University Press, 2001), by permission of Oxford University Press; and modified and reproduced by special permission of the publisher, CPP Inc., Mountain View, CA 94043, from *Introduction to Type* (R), Sixth Edition by Isabel Briggs Myers, Copyright 1998 and 2011 by Peter B. Myers and Katharine D. Myers, all rights reserved, further reproduction prohibited without the publisher's written consent.

17  In this regard, Jung was certainly influenced by the psychologist Alfred Binet, who made a distinction between two types of intellectual attitudes, 'externospection' and 'introspection'.

18  See *Man and His Symbols* by Carl G. Jung, edited by John Freeman (London: Dell Publishing, 1968), p 49.

19  See *The Collected Works of CG Jung*, edited by Herbert Read, Michael Fordham & Gerhard Adler (London: Routledge, 1953–78), Vol VI, paragraph 895.

20  Stevens, op cit, p 101.

21  This description of Rokeach's system of values is drawn from *Understanding Human Values: Individual and Societal*, a compilation volume edited by Milton Rokeach (New York: The Free Press, 1979).

22  See ibid, p 48, citing Kluckhohn (1951).

23  See ibid, p 48.

24  See *Change and Stability in American Value Systems 1968–1971* by Milton Rokeach, in ibid, pp 133–34.

25  See *From Individual to Institutional Values: With Special Reference to the Values of Science* by Milton Rokeach, in ibid, p 49.

26  *Values and the Organization: Suggestions for Research* by Patrick E. Connor and Boris W. Becker, in ibid, p 72.

27  See *Value Change Initiated by the Mass Media* by Keith R. Sanders and L. Erwin Atwood, in ibid, p 227.

28  See *Change and Stability in Values and Values Systems: A Sociological Perspective* by Robin M. Williams Jr, in ibid, pp 15–46.

### NOTES TO CHAPTER FOUR: A MAGICIAN FOR A GUIDE

1  See *The Archetypes and the Collective Unconscious* by Carl Jung (London: Routledge, 2002), p 285. Jung calls motifs such as the Hero and the Wise

Old Man 'archetypes'. Archetypes are an inherited collective of images, values and meaning to be found in every individual of every culture, he asserts, and we encounter these privileged symbols at moments of real significance in our lives, as we struggle to become our 'individuated' (separate) Self. Over the last two decades, the whole movement of psychoanalytic criticism, to which Jung's study of myths and legends belongs, has been contested vigorously. Nevertheless, archetypes continue to fascinate scholars, for these images exist in abundance in our cultural artefacts – see 'Literary Criticism and Psychoanalytic Positions' by Rainer Emig in *The Cambridge History of Literary Criticism, Volume 9, Twentieth-Century Historical, Philosophical and Psychological Perspectives*, edited by Christa Knellwolf and Christopher Norris (Cambridge: Cambridge University Press, 2001).

2  Occasionally, as the mythologist, Joseph Campbell, notes, the helper is a female figure – the Old Crone. Campbell, op cit, p 69.

3  Jung, *The Archetypes and the Collective Unconscious*, p 222.

4  Ibid, pp 217–18.

5  This is the first recorded use of the red dragon as a symbol of the Welsh, although it may have been used as a battle standard by the Welsh people as early as the fourth century.

6  'Merlinus' is the Latinised form of the name 'Myrddin'. Geoffrey of Monmouth changes one letter to avoid offending his prospective Norman-French readers, who would have associated 'Merdinus' with the vulgarism, *merde*.

7  See *The Study of Merlin in English Literature From the Middle Ages to the Present* by Christopher Dean (Lewiston: The Edwin Mellen Press, 1992) and *The New Arthurian Encyclopedia* edited by Norris J. Lacy et al (London: St James Press, 1991) to learn more about the literary figure of Merlin. The account provided here is drawn from these texts.

8  See *The Encyclopedia of Magic and Witchcraft* (London: Anness Publishing, 2002) and *The Anthropology of Magic* (Oxford: Berg, 2009) by Susan Greenwood to learn more about the history and practice of magic. The description provided here is drawn from these texts.

9  Peck, op cit, p 250–51

10  Ibid, p 131.

11  Ibid, p 133

12  Ibid, p 131.

13  See Mann, op cit.

14  Peck, op cit, p 58.

15  From *Helping: How to Offer, Give and Receive Help*, p 27, copyright © 2009 by Edgar H. Schein, Berrett-Koehler Publishers Inc., San Francisco, CA. All rights reserved.

16  Ibid, p 43.

17  Ibid, p 21.

18  Chungliang Al Huang and Jerry Lynch, *Mentoring: The Tao of Giving and Receiving Wisdom* (New York: HarperSanFrancisco, 1995), p 94. © 1995 by Chungliang Al Huang and Jerry Lynch. Reprinted by permission of Harper-Collins Publishers.

19  Peck, op cit, pp 250–51.

20  Schein, *Career Dynamics*, Chapters Three and Four.

21  Peck, op cit, p 148.

22  Huang and Lynch, op cit, p 76.

23  Schein, *Helping*, Chapter Three.

24  *Malory, Complete Works*, edited by Eugène Vinaver (Oxford: Oxford University Press, 1971), p 25.

25  Schein, *Helping*, p 32.

26  Huang and Lynch, op cit, p xi.

27  Schein, *Helping*, p 1.

28  Ibid.

### NOTES TO CHAPTER 5: THE FOREST OF ADVENTURE.

1  From *Perceval*, one of the trilogy of Arthurian romances called *Merlin and the Grail*, attributed to the French medieval writer, Robert de Boron and translated by Nigel Bryant (Cambridge: D.S. Brewer, 2001), p 143.

2  Kegan, op cit, p 114.

3  Durkin, op cit, p 85, citing Bowlby (1953).

4  Ibid, p 104.

5  As noted in Chapter Two of this book, as an infant's attachment to specific individuals becomes manifest, so his or her wariness in the presence of strangers also becomes apparent. As Durkin points out, however, this does not mean that young children are incapable of forming relationships with adults other than their parents. See Durkin, op cit, p 130.

6  See Durkin, op cit, pp 93–94, to learn more about attachments.

7  Ibid, p 97.

8  Kegan, op cit, pp 127–28.

9  Durkin, op cit, p 124, citing Kreppner (1992).

10  Three different patterns of parenting style have been identified by the developmental psychologist, Diana Baumrind. *Authoritarian* describes parents who obtain low scores on measures of emotional responsiveness and high scores on the control/demand dimension. *Authoritative* describes parents who obtain high scores on measures of both emotional responsiveness and control/demand; but, with regard to the latter, their emphasis is on fostering a sense of independent responsibility. *Permissive* describes parents who vary in terms of their position on the emotional continuum but all of whom have a

high level of tolerance for their offspring's impulses and activities. An *Authoritative* parenting style is associated with more favourable outcomes (which continue at least until middle childhood) on measures of self-esteem, autonomy, awareness of the feelings of others, and academic performance, leading to better adjusted and more popular children. See Durkin, op cit, pp 118–20.

11  See Durkin, op cit, Chapter Four.

12  Ibid, p 143.

13  Peck, op cit, pp 22–24.

14  Five types of children's social acceptance have been distinguished: popular children, whom many of their peers nominate or rate favourably as friends; rejected children, who are widely disliked; controversial children, who are regarded very favourably by some peers, but seen as disruptive by others; neglected, isolated children who are rarely nominated as friends; and average children, who are generally accepted and who do not receive extreme scores in peers' ratings. Durkin reports that securely attached, authoritatively parented children do seem to have an advantage in developing social relations, and that research also indicates that children who are rejected or who are unpopular at an early age will continue to experience negative social relations, miss out on the benefits of peer friendships, and be at greater risk of suffering in adulthood a host of developmental and psychosocial problems including alcoholism, social anxiety, depression, delinquency, educational failure and psychotism. See Durkin, op cit, p 146.

15  See Durkin, op cit, p 145, citing research by Asher and Parker (1989).

16  Ibid, p 530, citing Hill (1993).

17  Ibid, p 508, citing Lewin (1952).

18  Ibid, p 515.

19  Ibid, p 511.

20  Ibid, p 563.

21  Ibid, p 522, citing Ryan and Lynch (1989).

22  Family processes and peer relations are not the only risk factors which may lead to problem behaviours. Delinquency is multi-determined but research consistently demonstrates that maladaptive family systems and peer contexts are the key variables. See Durkin, op cit, Chapter 17.

23  Durkin, op cit, p 580, citing Brown (1990).

24  Ibid, pp 573–74.

25  Ibid, pp 523–24.

26  Kegan, op cit, p 129.

27  Ibid, p 222.

28  Durkin, op cit, p 545, citing Entwhistle (1990), Keating (1990), Marjoribanks (1979), and Roberts and Parsell (1989).

29 Ibid, pp 546–47, citing Lewin (1952), Verstraatan (1980), and de Volder and Lens (1982).

30 The career development theorist, Donald E. Super, has developed a stage theory of vocational self-concept which extends into late adulthood. "Super views adolescence as a crucial period in the development of vocational goals. He sees the mid-to-late teens as a period of crystallisation, during which the young person is formulating a vocational self-concept and narrowing down his or her options. This is followed by a stage of specification (in the late teens to early 20s) during which a specific choice is made." Durkin, op cit, p 549.

31 Ibid, pp 548–57.

32 See Diamond, op cit.

33 Preface to *Quantum Theory: A Very Short Introduction* by John Polkinghorne (Oxford: Oxford University Press, 2002). By permission of Oxford University Press.

34 Ibid, p 87.

35 See 'OD Morphogenesis: The Emerging Dialogic Platform of Premises' by Robert J. Marshak in *Practising Social Change* (online journal of the NTL Institute For Applied Behavioural Science), Edition 02, p 5.

36 Diamond, op cit, p 4.

37 Ibid.

### NOTES TO THE CONCLUSION

1 See *The Brain of the Firm* by Stafford Beer (Chichester: John Wiley and Sons, 1995), Second Edition, p 87.

2 See *Creating a Community of Inquiry: Conflict, Collaboration, Transformation* by William R. Torbert (London: John Wiley and Sons, 1976), Chapter Ten.

3 'Seven Transformations of Leadership' by David Rooke and William R. Torbert, *Harvard Business Review*, April 2005, p 3.

4 Torbert, op cit, p 149.

5 See Campbell, op cit.

6 A phrase drawn from Maslow's *Motivation and Personality*, op cit, and referenced in Chapters Two and Four of this book.

7 A phrase drawn from the Conclusion of *The Renaissance* by Walter Pater, and used in the Introduction of this book to describe the choice that is before us – to remain at the place we have reached now on our pathway of growth (i.e. to stop learning) or to continue to develop.

8 Lines from Alfred, Lord Tennyson's *Ulysses*. The first four lines of this extract are used in the Introduction of this book to describe the continuous journey of discovery which is available to us.

# The Pragmatism of Magic

✳

Kate Cowie has revitalised the idea that our progression along the human development pathway is grounded in a fundamental body of knowledge and practical application. She has also demonstrated, through the mythic figure, Merlin, the wisdom of helping others master the journey.

Merlin prepares kings and knights for great conquests by helping them develop 'heroic character' – physical strength, mental strength, and personal convictions that will serve them through life. He is referred to as a magician because he uses parables, prophecies and questions to haunt these heroes, stimulate their imagination, and lead them to create their own way, find their own answers. Merlin is the 'evocateur' – not the problem-solver – who facilitates what Cowie has identified as the primary agencies for change: transcendence and inclusion.

For professionals whose work is creating architectures for managing change, *Finding Merlin* is a fresh and timely guide. This book enjoins us to be imaginative during these times of crisis and opportunity. Can we see such world-changing forces as economic strife, globalisation, technological advances and shifting social values as opportunities for real change? And do we know how to work at the heart of chaos and organisation?

## *Where have all the Merlins gone?*

When I entered the field of organisation development, mentoring was the primary vehicle by which new practitioners were brought on board. Organisations such as the NTL Institute for Applied Behavioural Science provided both the training that was not otherwise available in formal curricula (the science) and the mentoring that nurtured practical skills (the art). Many of those mentors were like Merlin the magician. They employed a mystique that brought clarity and illumination. They worked from inner wisdom. They modelled purpose – seeking to make the world a better place by helping people be more effective and fulfilled in their life and work.

At a professional conference some thirty-five years ago, I met one of those mentoring icons, Herbert Allen Shepard. As I attempted to showcase my accomplishments, Herb listened intently. Then he asked me a question, "What do you want your next step to be?" This was a pivotal moment in my life, for it shifted me into a state of transcendent thinking that expanded the scope of my career tremendously.

Later on, at the Gestalt Institute of Cleveland (Gestalt Center of Organization and Systems Development), my teachers and mentors, notably John D. Carter, reinforced this transcendent way of thinking. Whenever I engaged them or my fellow students on important challenges, I walked away with a new thought to ponder – what the social-change activist Fran Peavey calls "a bigger and more provocative/meaningful question". Deeper inquiry continues to influence my performance, style and ability to support others to this day.

*What are the qualities of Merlin that we may aspire to?*
+ A presence that brings energy to those around.
+ A 'feel' – a connection to people, organisations, and situations.
+ Generative thinking, transcending what is known.
+ Letting go of mindsets that no longer serve their purpose.
+ Translating the deep intelligence of the collective into learning and action.
+ Creativity, play, dynamic imagination.
+ Courage to move through fear.
+ Investment in personal mastery as a life-long process.

*Some final integrating thoughts.*

In *The Learning Organization*, Peter Senge states that in situations of rapid change, only the organisations that are flexible, adaptive and productive will excel. In such organisations, people continually expand their capacity to create the results they truly desire; new and expansive patterns of thinking are nurtured; collective aspiration is set free; and people are continually learning to see the whole together.

Juanita Brown, co-founder of the World Café, describes how meaningful conversations enable us to notice a deeper pattern of connections: "As the network of new connections increases, knowledge sharing grows. The collective wisdom of the group becomes increasingly visible and accessible" (World Café prospectus 2008).

Fran Peavey states that what we know of life is only where we have decided to rest with our questioning; the skill lies in asking the questions that will make a difference (*By Life's Grace: Musings on the Essence of Social Change*, New Society Publishers, 1994).

'Using the Self' is described by Edwin Nevis, co-founder of the Gestalt Institute of Cleveland OSD Program and the Gestalt International Study Center, as acting upon one's observations, values, and feelings in order to have an effect on others; it is one of the most important skills of influence (*Organizational Consulting: A Gestalt Approach*, Gardner Press, 1987). Merlin's use of his Self as an instrument for change is a wonderful example of Nevis's premise.

If we can glean from this book and these sages the urgency to enrich and enjoy our own development, it will greatly enhance our ability to create conditions for unparalleled learning and change for individuals, organisations and society.

M. FRANCES BALDWIN